Best wi[shes in]
your own pursuit of
happiness.

Brian King

The 100 Day Promise

8/6/11
Keleigh & Justin~
We are so thrilled for you and the blessed occasion of your sealing in God's Holy Temple. Try to always remember the special feeling of love that you felt for each other as you knelt over the altar. Speaking from 22 years experience - Eternal Marriage is awesome. Have Fun! Love,
Joe, Erin, Justin, Rachel, Natalie, Brett & Shane Wilson

The 100 Day Promise:

Radically Transforming your Marriage by Living with Complete Concern for your Spouse's Happiness

Brian King

Introduction

In marriage, all couples face challenges whether brought on by themselves through the natural consequences of poor choices or through external events beyond their control. No matter the cause, we all decide at some point to either invest the effort to overcome our current circumstances or be content with mediocrity.

I am married to Nonnie. We've had wonderful experiences over the course of our ten years of marriage--much of which includes raising four great kids: Warren 8, Sterling 6, Morgan 5, and Bethanie 1. We've also had our challenges--also much of which includes raising four great kids. It was during one of these challenging times when we were returning home from a Thanksgiving weekend in Boston that led me to this 100 Day journey. We had an argument that bothered me so much that I could have gone the rest of the drive home without talking. I knew that doing so would start a negative downward cycle. I realized I would have to break out of it and muster the will to move us forward again. I sat there pondering many of the lessons I've learned over the years about how to have happy relationships. I remembered a thought I had when we were first married while in a similar frame of mind. It was a thought I believe came from God. "Just love her and let me do the teaching." I have remembered that from time to time over the years and have tried, but have not applied it as consistently as I could. I wondered what would happen if I not only broke out of this negative situation, but tried to act with the same selfless mindset for an extended period. So, I thought I'd try an experiment.

What if I just tried to love and serve her completely for 100 days? What would happen to me, her, our marriage, and our family?

The risks: There was the possibility that it would create a sense of servitude and that I would get walked over. Perhaps people who witnessed this experiment in action would think I was weak. Periodically, I joke that you have to "reset the bar" when the dynamics in a relationship get out of whack--when your wife expects too much. During this experiment, I would not be able to reset the bar. Lastly, what if it didn't change anything and I felt I had wasted my effort?

The benefits: Even if I didn't see the positive changes that I anticipated, I would have the benefit of exercising tremendous discipline and self-control, and become a better man, husband and father for it. However, I expect that love begets love and kindness and that there will be a positive change in our lives.

I promised myself that for 100 Days I would try to live with complete love and concern for my wife's happiness; I would show more gratitude and affection; I would help more without complaining and look for ways to proactively serve; I would listen more and "correct" less; and I would refrain from seeking justice and accuracy on some issues. I would have to leave some things unsaid, forgive more, and think unselfishly. If we had a disagreement, I would have to move forward in a positive way.

I found greater motivation to try this experiment as I remembered a special experience I had while visiting Nonnie's family before we were married and as I was preparing to buy an engagement ring. Things weren't going well and I was sitting in the living room with many of her family members coming and going. I was a little frustrated and trying to decide what I should do about my relationship with Nonnie. Her five-year old niece Rachel who was playing and running around, walked up to me and said, "You have to fight for love," and walked away. Why Rachel chose to say those words to me at that time, I do not know, but I do know that it taught me a great lesson. It really hit me directly. Fighting for love to me meant doing the things I am talking about here.

First, A short tribute to Nonnie: Who would want their behavior secretly documented for 100 Days?! Nonnie is an amazing woman and truly I am lucky to have her in my life. She has tremendous creativity and passion for the good in life. She amazes me with her desires to enrich the lives of our kids with wonderful opportunities and experiences. Nonnie is a person that people love to be around and trust. She has a unique talent to make people feel special and loved. I have seen her handle difficult situations in a way very few people could. She is extremely gracious, mannerly and thoughtful to people that we interact with. She is a very supportive wife. Nonnie believes in me and encourages me to reach my potential. She is not satisfied with a mediocre life and uses her imagination and our limited resources to make great things happen. Unfortunately for her, this book isn't about those things. Hopefully someday you will get to know the full story of how amazing she is. It is about my efforts to love her completely. Any family with four young kids is going to have their limits tested. This book is completely unfair to her in that it focuses only on the challenges and is only from my perspective.

Even though I tried to completely avoid arguments during these 100 Days, every relationship has to be able to have frank discussions about needs and expectations. Also, this experiment is not an endorsement of a one-sided balance of responsibilities. I don't think anyone, including myself, should constantly live as I tried to during this 100 days. By making this promise I aim to show the positive effects that love and kindness can have by taking it to the extreme for a short period of time. If the underlying mindset of love and concern for your spouse's happiness is woven into everything you do, then the benefits will come.

Day 1

Not too long after I made that commitment I received my first test. It was about 1:00am and we were driving home after a Thanksgiving holiday road trip. We had to pull off the highway to change Bethanie's diaper and we were both tired. There didn't appear to be an easy place to pull into so I said, "Should I just pull off the road or find a better place to park." Nonnie said, "Would you just make a decision, you don't have to ask me about everything." The journey of a thousand miles begins with a single step. (Chinese Proverb)

The surest sign of wisdom is happiness.

-Michel de Montaigne

Day 2

We arrived home at 4:00am extremely tired. I carried in the kids and luggage from the car and let Nonnie go straight to bed. A few hours later when the kids were awake I got up, let her sleep, and fed the baby, etc. since she had been driving the last leg of the journey.

Throughout the day I gave a lot of positive comments and a couple hugs. One time she even knew I was overdoing it and raised an eyebrow at me. I smiled and laughed a little, wondering how she would react as the days went on.

Day-to-day acts of service…may not seem important, but they are building cords of love that become so strong they can seldom be broken.

Marvin J. Ashton

Day 3

On my way home we had a fun phone conversation talking about birthday plans and a trip to the dentist for the kids. Nonnie mentioned a new program she was going to try as an incentive for the kids to do nice things for each other. I resisted the urge to ask how much the related items were going to cost and why we need another program and said something positive.

I came home early from work so I could help with the kids and the house, especially in light of us still recovering from our trip. She recognized what I had done and appreciated it. After we worked for a few hours I said, "Why don't I put the kids to bed and you take a break."

Kindness trumps greed: it asks for sharing. Kindness trumps fear: it calls forth gratefulness and love. Kindness trumps even stupidity, for with sharing and love, one learns.
-Marc Estrin

Day 4

Normally when I come home from Cub Scouts I am rushing to get ready to go play basketball. While I was changing clothes Nonnie asked if I could help her with something downstairs. I said sure…why don't I just stay home tonight and help you with "stuff" around here. She just lit up and said "No, you should still go, I just needed your help moving something." I still stayed home and helped out a little extra. I also told her later how grateful I was for all the hard work she does for our family.

Remember not only to say the right thing in the right place, but far more difficult still, to leave unsaid the wrong thing at the tempting moment.

Benjamin Franklin

Day 5

When I was driving home from work I thought, "What can I do when I get home that will make Nonnie really happy?" I thought I should ask her how her day was and be interested in the events of her day rather than only talking about what was on my mind. When I asked she seemed pleased, but we were cut short by the kids.

She asked if she could go exercise while I watched the kids and put them to bed. I said "of course," and then gave her a big hug and kiss.

When I told Nonnie about how busy my day was going to be tomorrow she said that she'd have to help me get to bed early so I would be ready for it. Although it isn't too unusual for her to help me with my big projects, I couldn't help but think that my extra effort toward being unselfish was making it easier for her to think that way as well.

I cleaned the dishes and helped the kids straighten up, then put them to bed. I made Nonnie some hot chocolate. When I brought it to her she was on the phone, but lit up with a huge smile and mouthed, "Thank You!"

Freedom is that instant between when someone tells you to do something and when you decide how to respond.

-Jeffrey Borenstein

Day 6

Nonnie asked what name I gave her on my cell phone, since I had programmed my name in her cell phone as "Genius." She was disappointed that her number wasn't even in my phone. I told her I only programmed the numbers that I couldn't remember. Today I showed her that I programmed her name in my phone as "Happiness."

Nonnie has wanted an island for the kitchen and for over a year has had a picture of the one she wanted on the refrigerator. I was already planning to get it for Christmas. She called me today and said she found one she liked and that the price was lower than the one we planned on buying. I told her to definitely get it. She called me back and asked if I was glad we bought it. I told her I was mainly happy that she was happy. She thought that was really nice.

When I was driving home in traffic Nonnie told me to hurry because she was going to a PTA meeting at 6:30pm. I chose not to tell her that if she would have told me about it sooner I could have tried to leave a few minutes earlier. Instead I said, "Sure, I'll do the best I can."

I was tired and getting ready to go to bed. I realized my shoes were downstairs and went to go get them to make sure I had everything ready for the morning. When I went downstairs I noticed two empty suitcases near the door to the basement, apparently put there so they could be carried down to the storage room at some point. I stood there for a few seconds then decided to go ahead and take them down. When I got downstairs Nonnie was watching TV. She said, "Why don't you come sit here for a minute," with a warm smile. Then we kissed.

Once a man has made a commitment to a way of life, he puts the greatest strength in the world behind him. It's something we call heart power. Once a man has made this commitment, nothing will stop him short of success.

-Vincent "Vince" Lombardi

Day 7

Tonight when I was helping get dinner ready I noticed the salad did not look very good. It appeared to be made of only the parts of the lettuce that I normally throw away. I started to say something about it, then stopped.

We had some friends stop by and Nonnie was starting to tell them the *amazing* story about the island we just bought for the kitchen. I almost interjected to say something about how the story really isn't that interesting, but decided not to.

After the kids were in bed I said, "Why don't I do the dishes while you go take a break?" She said thanks but she would stay in the kitchen with me and talk while she ate and took care of other odds and ends.

To love someone means to see him as God intended him...

-Fyodor Dostoyevsky

Day 8

This morning we were upstairs cleaning and Nonnie said she wanted to show me the new comforter she bought and went into a long story about how she was so lucky to get it at the store and that it is just the perfect design etc. She said it is for a King size bed (which we don't have) but plan to get someday. I said, "Nonnie, I am glad you found one that you like. I like it too. I am worried, though, that we're beginning to go a little too far from our weekly budget and hope we can try to stay on track going forward." She said, "Well, I thought I did a great job," (in finding the right one at a great price) and showed some resentment as she turned away. I can't remember what I said, but I remember getting her to smile as I hugged her and kissed her on the cheek.

No kind action ever stops with itself. One kind action leads to another. Good example is followed. A single act of kindness throws out roots in all directions, and the roots spring up and make new trees. The greatest work that kindness does to others is that it makes them kind themselves.

-Amelia Earhart

Day 9

Last night my sons (who were supposed to be in bed) came to us and said they saw some teenagers steal the carrot off of the snowman we made. When I checked the carrot was still there but the pipe was gone. I quickly went down the street and approached a group of about 12 teenagers and asked them if they knew where the pipe went and they said, "No." I told them someone told me they saw them take it. I knew who a few of the kids were and they said they didn't know anything about it. They didn't seem to be lying, but I couldn't tell for sure. I thought it was possible the pipe fell out earlier. Nonnie was positive it was them and was already thinking how terrible those boys were. I debated the lack of certainty about the situation and said I was about 50-50. In the morning the pipe was found in the snow under the front of the snowman. I resisted the urge to rub it in.

I told her how great she looked today and how impressed I was with how much she accomplished. I worked hard throughout the day taking care of the kids, especially the baby, in the way she wants it. "Serve them the way they want to be served," a favorite saying around our house. I let her take a nap while I handled things and cleaned the kitchen. I made her a cup of hot chocolate. Later in the afternoon/evening she came to me and said I should take a nap and have time to prepare to teach my class which I really appreciated.

When we were eating dinner I said to all the kids, "Raise your hand if you have the best mom in the world." They all raised their hands and called out "I do!"

Forgiveness is not an occasional act: it is an attitude.

-Martin Luther King, Jr

Day 10

We went to Walmart to get a Christmas tree. She said she wanted to pick up a few things while we were there. After we started walking into the store Nonnie said it would go a lot faster if I stayed with the kids while she did the shopping. I stayed with the kids for a really long time in the toy area. When she came back I didn't complain about how long she left us waiting.

I asked Nonnie if she would like her feet rubbed with lotion and she said, "Oh, that would be soooo nice."

As we were getting ready for bed she asked me if I would go get her a cup of ice water. Rather than mumbling something or joking about how she is taking years off of my life I just said, "Sure."

People from a planet without flowers would think we must be mad with joy the whole time to have such things about us.

-Iris Murdoch

Day 11

I was planning on taking the Cub Scouts to a local museum tonight. I realized this afternoon that it wasn't open late enough. Nonnie called and asked about my plans and I told her my predicament. She offered to help and found a great craft for them to make as Christmas presents for their families. I told her how grateful I was.

When I was leaving for scouts she asked if I could pick up some things at the store on the way home, "if that is OK." I told her that was a really nice way to ask.

At the store I bought her a bouquet of flowers and put them in a vase. After I remembered that I forgot to bring home the sandwich she asked me to bring and realized the restaurant was now closed. I offered to make her something else. She finally said yes and even though she was disappointed she quickly got over it. The flowers helped.

Real giving is when we give to our spouses what's important to them, whether we understand it, like it, agree with it, or not.

-Michele Weiner-Davis

Day 12

As soon as I arrived home she asked me to put up the Christmas decorations outside. I didn't make much of a fuss, changed clothes and took care of it. While we were making and feeding the kids dinner I gave her a hug and a kiss.

After dinner I helped the kids empty the dishwasher, cleanup and take out the trash. Nonnie asked me to pull the plants out of the pots on our front porch. I wasn't excited about getting new plants for the porch. I made a mild comment about how I wasn't very excited about that, but I did it anyway.

I can live for two months on a good compliment.

-Mark Twain

Day 13

On the way home from work Nonnie asked me to pick up new rosemary Christmas trees at Lowes. I reminded her how I didn't like having to get new plants every few months for the porch and (half joking) that in order for me to be the one to actually go pick them up I would have to swallow a lot of pride. She laughed and said that it would mean so much more to her then. I picked them up.

When I got home I stood under the mistletoe in the doorway and said, pointing into the dining room, "Nonnie, what is that?" When she came over to look I gave her a big kiss. She lit up with a bright smile.

She went to a book club while I cleaned up the kitchen, got the kids ready for bed, and read to them.

Last night when I had put the Christmas lights up they didn't come on when I plugged them in and I realized it was a problem with the outlets. Nonnie was really anxious for me to get them fixed. I told her I would work on it today. When she went to the book club tonight I was able to fix the outlets and have the lights on for her when she came home. She was very excited to see them on when she arrived and thanked me.

Stretching our souls in service helps us to rise above our cares, concerns, and challenges. As we focus our energies on lifting the burdens of others, something miraculous happens. Our own burdens diminish. We become happier. There is more substance to our lives.
-David S. Baxter

Day 14

This morning before I left for work while everyone was still asleep I found the video on YouTube of the Zac Brown Band song, "Whatever It Is" and emailed it to Nonnie. She called me this morning and told me how romantic it was, especially after I explained how I sent it this morning because I wanted her to get it when I wasn't home.

When Nonnie called me on the way home from work I said, "Hi Pretty Lady." She said she liked it better when I called her "Happiness" as I have a few times since I gave her that name on my phone. She asked me to pick up the movie "Julie and Julia" for us to watch tonight. After I picked it up she called me and I explained how it looked like the most painfully boring movie for a man to watch. She said she would make it up to me.

When I came home I tricked her into coming under the mistletoe again and kissed her. Later on while we were feeding the kids I hugged her and said to the kids, "Do you realize how lucky you guys are to have such an amazing mother!?"

When we were starting the movie I sat down next to her on the couch and said in a playful manner, "I don't understand why I like you so much! I wish I could shake this spell you've cast over me." She just smiled.

Right actions in the future are the best apologies for bad actions in the past.

-Tryon Edwards

Day 15

There wasn't anything too dramatic or noteworthy today. We were up really late last night and when the baby woke in the morning I got up and let Nonnie sleep a little longer. We worked really hard around the house cleaning up and taking care of a variety of Christmas projects. Holding myself accountable by writing down how I did each day makes it easier to remember the promise and consistently put forth the effort. If I wasn't holding myself accountable each day I'm sure I wouldn't give enough effort to make it work.

That best portion of a good man's life; His little, nameless, unremembered acts of kindness and of love.

-William Wordsworth

Day 16

I must say things have been great between Nonnie and me lately. We're hugging, kissing and joking a lot more than we have been in long time. This morning I got up with the baby so she could sleep a little longer.

I stayed home from church because Sterling was sick. When they came home I had the kitchen clean and lunch was on the stove. I offered to help her carry her things in from the car and told her how pretty she looked.

Nonnie invited some friends over for lunch while she was at church. I refrained from complaining about the late notice and just casually asked about her motivations. We worked really hard to get everything ready.

Be kind for everyone you meet is fighting a great battle.

-Philo of Alexandria

Day 17

Nonnie went to run some errands after I came home from work and was taking a lot longer than I expected. When she called I said, "Hello Sadness." She laughed and asked, "Are you mad? I said, "A little but I'm choosing not to make a big deal out of it." When she came home she was really happy with all the things we had done, including teaching Morgan how to ride a bike.

Just after we put the kids to bed I said, "What can I do to help you?" She said, "Just look around," in a way that bothered me, but I chose not to react.

I asked her if we could start saying a prayer together before we go to bed. She was really happy and said she loved the idea.

Try praising your wife, even if it does frighten her at first.

-Billy Sunday

Day 18

This morning before I left for work I sent an email to Nonnie saying that I came across this quote and really liked it:

"Love is a temporary madness. It erupts like an earthquake and then subsides. And when it subsides you have to make a decision. You have to work out whether your roots have become so entwined together that it is inconceivable that you should ever part. Because this is what love is. Love is not breathlessness, it is not excitement, it is not the promulgation of promises of eternal passion. That is just being "in love" which any of us can convince ourselves we are. Love itself is what is left over when being in love has burned away, and this is both an art and a fortunate accident. Your mother and I had it, we had roots that grew towards each other underground, and when all the pretty blossom had fallen from our branches we found that we were one tree and not two." -St. Augustine from the movie Captain Corelli's Mandolin

She didn't say anything about it after we talked on the phone when I was at work. When I was driving home I asked her if she liked the quote, partially worried that perhaps she could have misinterpreted it to mean I wasn't in love anymore or something like that. She said she liked it, but was wondering if I was going to die or something. I said, "What do you mean?" She said because you're being really nice lately. I said, "That's really funny that you said that." And then we talked about something else. I was really amused by her saying this and thought about how it didn't really take a lot more effort than how I had been living. It was mainly just living with a different mindset. I wondered what she must be thinking was causing me to do some of these extra things.

Nonnie was really kind and helped me prepare something for Cub Scouts. When I came home she said that I should take a break and that she was going to take care of me tonight and that I should take a bubble bath or something. No, I didn't take a bubble bath but we had a nice night relaxing. We said a prayer together before bed. I also gave her a foot massage.

Any man worth his salt will stick up for what he believes is right, but it takes a slightly better man to acknowledge instantly and without reservation that he is in error.

-Andrew Jackson

Day 19

I made her really happy when I told her I was taking the day off. She had been asking me if I could come to Morgan's preschool performance and I had been saying I'll see how it looks when we get closer. When I said I was taking the whole day off so I could come to the performance, get the car fixed, and do a few other things around the house she was pleased.

I started the morning around 6:30am, getting up with the baby, then fixing breakfast for the kids, and letting Nonnie sleep until around 7:30am. I sent the kids upstairs to take her breakfast in bed.

This morning we had some confusion about who would watch the baby in the bathtub. I asked Warren to watch the baby for a couple minutes. A minute later the baby was crawling on the floor. We disagreed for a minute about what had happened and about five minutes later I came to her and said I was sorry I didn't handle the whole situation better. She said she also could have handled it better.

We heard around 6:20pm that the car was ready to be picked up from the repair shop. It was approximately 20 minutes away, sometimes more, and the shop closes at 7:00pm. I said, OK, let's go get it. She said, we need to feed the kids first. I said, "Nonnie, we will not have time to feed them and still get the car. If they weren't saying they were hungry now, surely they can survive for 40 minutes. Plus, we need the car for tomorrow." She said in frustration, "Why, do you always do this?" I said, "Always do what?" And that was it, we went and picked up the car.

I have been under a tight deadline to grade a lot of research papers tonight and as the evening progressed I became frustrated that I was getting interrupted. After I calmly explained the situation she seemed to understand. She came up later with a couple grilled cheese sandwiches and a cup of yogurt. I was very grateful. A few hours later I came out of the office for something and she asked how it was going. I told her I'd be up until around 1:00am. She asked if there was anything she could do. I asked for a bowl of ice cream and she said, "OK."

And whosoever shall compel thee to go a mile, go with him twain.

-Jesus, Matthew 5:41

Day 20

One of the critical skills to having a good relationship is to be able to get over minor disagreements or bad moments quickly and move forward without bringing the negative experience into the future. Nonnie wanted to get our family pictures taken at a religious visitor's center with Christmas trees inside. I wasn't excited about it. On the way into the building I said that I hope we can do this as reverently and discretely as possible. It was hard to get the camera lighting and the four kids situated just right and it was taking a lot longer than I felt comfortable with. My concern about being a distraction increased as the relentless struggle to get the right picture continued and we moved to different

spots to try again. After very reluctantly agreeing to "just one more picture" over and over again, I finally walked away with the kids. As I was sitting there frustrated, I heard a narration of Jesus' words from the speaker say, "Walk in the meekness of my Spirit and you shall find peace." I thought about the statement and wondered what more could have been done to improve the situation. When it was over we disagreed about how bad the situation was, but I decided to put it behind me.

True heroism is remarkably sober, very undramatic. It is not the courage to surpass others at whatever cost, but the courage to serve others at whatever the cost.

-Arthur Ashe

Day 21

This morning while I was getting ready for work in the bathroom around 5:45am I heard the baby crying and Nonnie got up to get her. A few minutes later she came in the bathroom with the baby and asked me if I knew where the pacifier was. I said that I didn't but that after I was ready in a couple minutes I would go out to the car to help her look for it. She then gave a very sincere apology for how she acted last night. I said I understood and that it was all right. She asked for a kiss and we kissed.

She called me at work saying she was sick and had just thrown up and asked if I could come home early. I told her to wait an hour and if she still felt bad I would come home. In a hour she said she was still sick. It was only a couple of hours early and I could have told her to just hang on a little longer and I'll be home. However, I thought she would really appreciate the help, so I arranged to come home early. She called me when I was in the car and said how grateful she was.

If we keep doing what we're doing, we're going to keep getting what we're getting.

-Steven R Covey

Day 22

One of our kids came in at 5:00am saying they had wet the bed. I got up and handled it. When the baby started crying at 6:30am I said I would handle it. Nonnie said she would take care of it and then let me sleep until 9:30am! I needed it so much and was so thankful. I tricked her again into coming near the dining room and kissed her under the mistletoe.

We had a snowstorm today with about 20 inches of snow. I went out in the afternoon with the kids. We went sledding, dug in the snow drifts and marched around in the mounds of snow. I cleaned off the trampoline and the cars and started shoveling the driveway. I intended to make a snow igloo so I threw the snow in a pile on one side of the driveway. As we got further away from the pile I filled up a large trashcan with snow and dumped it in our pile. I eventually had four neighborhood kids helping me as our kids went inside. Nonnie asked me to come in and I walked over and said, "I've got four kids shoveling my driveway, I am not going in right now, with a smile on my face. I was out for another half hour and we had a massive pile of snow ready for our igloo. I coached some of them in the digging while I put things away and cleaned the cars again. When I went inside Nonnie was a little upset that I had spent so much time outside. I explained a little what I was thinking and then just tried to move forward in a positive way. She seemed to get over it soon.

If you want others to be happy, practice compassion. If you want to be happy, practice compassion.

-Tenzin Gyatso, 14th Dalai Lama

Day 23

I got up first with the baby this morning and fed her. Today was pretty nice. I worked more on shoveling the driveway and building an igloo with the kids. It was getting closer to the time we were supposed to go to our friend's house for dinner. I went upstairs and she was resting. Rather than telling her how late we were and how she better get moving, I just laid down next to her. When she opened her eyes I just let the conversation go towards our dinner plans and suggested a plan for us to move forward. I didn't rush her and just helped get the kids ready. We left in separate cars and when I went outside with the three older kids I realized how icy the sidewalk was. I thought of how bad it would be if Nonnie slipped on the ice and went back inside and warned her to be extra careful when she went outside. I arrived about 20 minutes before her.

The food seemed to be going fast so I made a plate for Nonnie and set it aside for her. When she came I fed the baby and took care of her most of the time we were there, except when other kids were holding her. When it was getting close to time to leave the party I asked her if she was close enough to leave for me to round up the kids. She said yes and I went and had the kids clean up, say goodbye to everyone and then get their shoes on. Nonnie took about another 20 minutes in different conversations and I waited to leave as the kids swirled around me. I gently tried to encourage her but didn't make too much of a fuss and didn't let myself get angry. As we were walking out I said I probably shouldn't have gotten the kids ready so soon and she said she was sorry. When we arrived home she wanted to take a walk around the side of the house because she said the snow was so romantic. We walked hand in hand through snow and laughed about a couple things and then realized we needed to get inside to take care of our kids.

    We stayed up late working on our family Christmas card. I thought her ideas were really clever and told her she was an excellent writer.

Giving frees us from the familiar territory of our needs by opening our mind to the unexplained worlds occupied by the needs of others.

-Barbara Bush

Day 24

Last night the printer ran out of ink so she asked if I would go get a new print cartridge and stamps. I came back with daisies that I thought she would like. When she has been asking me to do things she has been asking with more respect and consideration, such as, "When you're finished" or "After you have a chance to relax."

When I passed her reading a book I thought she looked beautiful. I said, "Man, people must really think I am a vain person for marrying someone as pretty as you." She said, "Oh, please" as though I was overdoing it, but had a smile on her face that said she didn't mind the compliment.

We were both tired from a long day. I was home from work because of the icy/snowy roads and spent the day shoveling snow, printing/folding Christmas letters, running errands and preparing for Morgan's birthday party. Luckily she hasn't seen me working on the laptop writing this down too often. When she does I just let on that I'm playing a computer game.

Gratitude is a mark of a noble soul and a refined character. We like to be around those who are grateful. They tend to brighten all around them. They make others feel better about themselves. They tend to be more humble, more joyful, more likable.

-Joseph B. Wirthlin

Day 25

This morning as I was getting ready for work Nonnie came in the bathroom and thanked me for handling the kids last night. She also thanked me for the flowers and said it was especially meaningful with everything I had on my mind I still thought to buy flowers. When I came home from work I resisted the urge to complain about every light in the house being on and how we have way too much perishable food in our refrigerator (three loafs of bread, unopened gallon of milk, eight yogurts, etc.) even though I asked her not to buy too much before our trip. Being a California girl she likely just thought we needed more because of the snowstorm.

We brought Christmas treats to our neighbors tonight that involved cherries. Nonnie wanted us all to sing "We wish you a cherry Christmas." I mildly questioned this but didn't want to discuss it in front of the kids, so I asked her if I could talk to her alone. As we went around the corner I reasoned that it was strange enough for our neighbors to see us singing to them, let alone us singing "a cherry Christmas." We agreed to just sing the first part of the regular version that ends, "and a Happy New Year."

I was watching a football game that I really wanted to watch. It was getting late and we had to prepare for the trip we were taking tomorrow. Nonnie really wanted to watch a movie that we had borrowed and that she has been talking about all week. In the third quarter I said I wouldn't mind turning it off so she can watch her movie. She thanked me, but said I could finish my game. During the second half I rubbed her back.

Tomorrow will bring a serious challenge to my 100 day challenge. We are leaving tomorrow morning on a 15 hour road trip to my parents home for

Christmas. We have been on many fun trips to many different states and countries (including Bahrain, UAE, Morocco, Spain, and Portugal). I know we are going to have a great time, but packing for the trip and being in close quarters with four young kids for so long will inevitably take a lot of effort and require patience and compromise.

Anything that we learn to do we learn by the actual doing of it…we become just by doing just acts, temperate by doing temperate ones, brave by doing brave ones.

-Aristotle

Day 26

We stayed up until 2:30am and I was up at 6am with the baby. We worked and worked throughout the day. We did mounds of laundry. Around 12:00pm I was getting anxious to leave because I heard a storm was coming and I didn't want to leave too much of the trip until the second day. When I saw Nonnie doing things like folding dishtowels I asked if she wouldn't mind leaving some things like that until we returned. I don't remember what her answer was but it was noncommittal. Later in the afternoon when I checked my email Nonnie was frustrated that I wasn't making progress toward leaving. Rather than arguing I just said I'd get back to work.

I made a couple wrong turns. One was missing the turnoff when the highway split and another was getting off at the wrong exit for the hotel. She was very patient about both mistakes. The first half of the journey was over, the kids were good, I was tired, but we had a great time.

In a controversy the instant we feel anger we have already ceased striving for the truth, and have begun striving for ourselves.

-Buddha

Day 27

    I took the three older kids down for breakfast and then came back to the room to pack up. We stopped off at Walmart to get "a couple things" that we needed for two people's gifts. We were there for a really long time and she asked me whether we should buy several things that I didn't think we needed such as a book, "How to Make the Best Christmas." I thought this was funny because in the mood I was in not asking me to buy that book would have made for a better Christmas. I tried not to be too negative and just gently move things along.

    When we got to my parents house around 7:30pm Christmas Eve I brought things in from the car and asked Nonnie what she needed done to get settled. We had fun later that night talking to my parents and wrapping Christmas presents. Around 1:00am we were finished and I dressed up in a Santa suit and she woke the kids up to sneak a peak at Santa.

The greatest discovery of my generation is that human beings can alter their lives by altering their attitudes of mind.

William James

Day 28

The three older kids were up at 6:00am and I got up with them so Nonnie, Bethanie, and my parents could sleep in. They all woke up around 7:40am. and we had a great Christmas morning. I was reminded again how the "true spirit of Christmas," which is to give and live unselfishly, is what this 100 day promise is really about.

Later Nonnie asked me to go get her something at the store that guys don't like to buy since she didn't know the area and I did it without complaint. She mentioned later how nice it was for me to do that especially considering it was snowing outside.

The real act of marriage takes place in the heart, not in the ballroom or church or synagogue. It's a choice you make -- not just on your wedding day, but over and over again -- and that choice is reflected in the way you treat your husband or wife.

-Barbara De Angelis

Day 29

Later tonight Nonnie asked me to throw her a blanket while I was laying on the floor in front of the TV. Instead of just throwing it to her I got up and laid the blanket on her and tucked her in which made her smile. Perhaps it is just doing that little extra to make her smile that makes all the difference.

You don't marry one person; you marry three: the person you think they are, the person they are, and the person they are going to become as a result of being married to you.

-Richard Needham

Day 30

The bedroom at my parent's house where we were staying was in the basement. The basement is where the pool table is and where the kids like to play. I knew that my young kids and nieces/nephews would need reminders so when the baby was napping I reminded them a few times to try to be a little quieter. Bethanie started to stir from her nap. Nonnie came downstairs and said I should try to keep it quieter and I explained that I had made an effort but would try harder.

My sister Stefanie, her husband Chris, Nonnie and I wanted to go to the movies so we decided one of us would watch an animated show with the kids while the other three watched something we wanted to watch in a different theater. I offered to go with the kids. Nonnie was kind to say that she would do it and said she wanted me to be able to see what I wanted. Stefanie ended up convincing Nonnie that she (Stefanie) should go with the kids.

Gratitude unlocks the fullness of life. It turns what we have into enough, and more. It turns denial into acceptance, chaos into order, confusion into clarity...Gratitude makes sense of our past, brings peace for today and creates a vision for tomorrow.

-Melodie Beattie

Day 31

I offered a few times throughout the day to help her with things she was working on or just asked if there was anything I could do for her.

I overheard Nonnie telling a few of my family members how I always compliment her and tell the kids how lucky they are to have her as a mother and how much she appreciates that.

Love is never wasted, for its value does not rest upon reciprocity.

-Neal A. Maxwell

Day 32

I got up with the baby at 6:30am this morning to feed her and made pancakes for the rest of the extended family around 8:00am. Nonnie got up later and thanked me for letting her sleep.

I told Nonnie on the way home from lunch, "Man, I am so lucky. My wife is so much fun, the life of the party, beautiful, smart, a great wife and mother. I've got the total package!" She just had a big smile on her face.

She told me that she didn't think she would go shopping this afternoon so that she could stay home and watch the kids while I slept. I told her that made me really happy that she would offer to do that, but that I really wanted her to go out with my mom, sisters and sisters-in-law.

Do you know the difference between involvement and commitment? Think of ham and eggs. The chicken is involved. The pig is committed.

-Martina Navratilova

Day 33

We had to go to the emergency care center for Bethanie. We wanted to keep her out of the waiting room so I waited inside while Nonnie and the baby waited in the car. She was going to go a block down the street and then come back and wait. We thought it would take at least 30 minutes so I assumed she would be back in time. After about 45 minutes they called for Bethanie and I went out and the car wasn't there. I called her and she said she was four minutes away. She explained that she had been driving around to settle down the baby. We lost our place in line and had to wait another 20 minutes or so. I calmly explained that I thought she'd be back and what the new situation was but didn't get frustrated.

Tonight Nonnie went to the old Dairy Queen where I used to work and told them I used to work there and that if I am any indication of what happens to people who work there they have great things in their future.

Let's try to remember that love means keeping in touch with each other's thoughts and feelings...listening, not just to words, but to the emotions behind them...seeing, not just the smiles and frowns, but the hurts and pleasures that causes them.

-Unknown

Day 34

This morning we both got up around 8:30am. She got in the shower and I took care of the kids. Around 10:30am she took a nap. I took care of the baby and kept an eye on my three other kids. When she woke up I realized that it was almost time to leave for a family activity and that I hadn't fed the kids. She was disappointed but we didn't make a big issue of it. I periodically asked if I could help her and what she wanted to do that day.

Nonnie told my brother-in-law Chris how much she wanted to go to Costa Rica for our tenth anniversary. He travels there periodically for his work and said he might be able to get us a good deal on parts of the trip. Later she asked me what I thought about it. I said that if we could arrange it in the budget I'd be happy to do it, even though I wasn't as excited about it as she was.

Reply when asked if he had ever been wrong...Yes, once – many, many years ago. I thought I had made a wrong decision. Of course, it turned out that I had been right all along. But I was wrong to have thought that I was wrong.

-John Foster Dulles

Day 35

Today we spent until 2:00pm getting ready for the day, cleaning and packing to leave. It went rather smoothly since we weren't in a hurry and I refrained from pointing out what I thought were better ways of doing little things. We had both gotten up around 8:30am and she kindly asked if I would take care of the kids and make breakfast while she got ready and started packing. At one point on the road I said, "I sure wouldn't mind snuggling up with you and kissing you."

Nonnie was reading a book about parenting and families when we were in the car. She told me about a part that talked about how children that aren't allowed to make their own decisions when they are young aren't able to make good decisions when they are teenagers. I said something about what I liked about how my family implemented that. She thought it sounded like I was criticizing her family and we debated it a little. We didn't come to any agreement but after a few minutes I forgot about it and we talked about other things.

We decided to make a detour and go through Nashville without doing any preparation in terms of knowing where the significant sites were. I was picturing just pulling off the highway, picking up a few souvenirs and taking a few photos in front of some of the music halls. When we arrived in Nashville we stopped off at the "Travel Center" thinking it was a tourist welcome center. I went in to get some information and realized it was just a truck stop. When I came back to the car and told Nonnie she was disappointed. I said I would just run back into the store and see if I could buy a map. It took longer than I expected and I found out we were in the wrong area. It was getting late, the kids were tired, so I drove fast and missed the exit. It took a long time to turn around and I tried to be as patient as I could under the tension and joked about whether we should sign up for the TV show, The Amazing Race.

It is only imperfection that complains of what is imperfect. The more perfect we are, the more gentle and quiet we become towards the defects of others.

-Joseph Addison

Day 36

We checked out of the hotel and started out on an eleven-hour journey. It was a tough trek in the cold rain with a lot of stops for potty breaks, dirty diapers, and eating. Nonnie saw a sign for the Biltmore Estate and asked if we could go. At one of the stops I looked at the map and saw that it would be about an hour and a half detour to Ashville. I explained that to her and then asked her if she still wanted to do it. After she explained that she did I agreed without hesitation because I thought she would really enjoy it. On our way we were forced on a detour that sent us back the same way we came because of rock slides. Apparently we, and many others, missed the signs that supposedly explained this. She was disappointed but seemed to stay positive. We didn't end up going because when we called we found out they would already be closed for the day.

When we were almost home I told her she passed the road trip test. She didn't know what a road trip test was. I explained that when you're dating someone or evaluating someone there is a thing called the road trip test where you see what someone is really like by being around them for a long time in confined spaces and trying circumstances. I explained that she handled our challenges very well and was very pleasant to be around.

We arrived home around 11:30pm on New Years Eve. We had the kids in bed around 11:50pm and we were both very tired as we sat down in front of the TV. I asked her if she would like me to make her something. She said, "Yes, that would be great." After I brought it she was very thankful. We enjoyed a nice time watching the New Years Eve celebrations on TV and hugged and kissed.

Where there is great love, there are always miracles.

-Willa Cather

Day 37

I knew today had a lot of work in store for us. We had left the house in a pretty rough condition, had to put away everything from our trip, and put away all the Christmas decorations. When I woke up I told her that I was ready to work and just let me know what she wanted done. I also mentioned a few things I wanted to get done if there was time.

Nonnie wanted us to go on a walk so we finished our game and after I asked them to put their shoes and coats on we threw a couple balls at each other for a few minutes. We disagreed about what needed to get done so we could leave. A few minutes later I apologized and hugged her and kissed her on the cheek. She was happy and thanked me.

It was after 1:00am and we were getting ready for bed upstairs and I was on the computer. She came in and said her head hurt or something and asked if I could go get her a drink of ice water and added, "Whenever you're done there on your way to bed." I said, "Sure."

For one human being to love another; that is perhaps the most difficult of our tasks; the ultimate, the last test and proof; the work for which all other work is but preparation.

-Rainer Maria Rilke

Day 38

  Nonnie told me about a chess class she had signed Warren up for and I said, "I'm fine with him being signed up for chess, in general though, I'd prefer you talk about things like this with me before you do it." She said, "OK."

  I readily agreed to let Nonnie and Morgan go to a movie with some friends. While she was gone I fixed the leaky bathroom sink, repaired the garage door opener by replacing a new part I had ordered, organized the garage so she could park her car inside, and cleaned the kitchen, in addition to taking care of the three other kids. When she came back she was very happy that I was able to get so much done.

  After the kids were in bed Nonnie worked on her presentation for church tomorrow. I helped her a couple times when she asked me. I came back later and rubbed her shoulders and asked if there was anything else I could do to help her and if she wanted me to make her something to eat.

Love is like a campfire: It may be sparked quickly, and at first the kindling throws out a lot of heat, but it burns out quickly. For long lasting, steady warmth (with delightful bursts of intense heat from time to time), you must carefully tend the fire.

-Molleen Matsumara

Day 39

Tonight I said to Nonnie, "How would you like to go on a date with me this weekend." Almost everything we have done socially for a long time has been events that we have been invited to. She beamed a smile and asked, "Really, do you have something in mind?" I said I could put something together. She said, "I have an idea, why don't we alternate weekends planning a date." I said that sounded great.

I told her I really liked her a lot and joked about this inexplicable feeling I have that doesn't make any sense that makes me want to hug and kiss her. As I think about how things have gone so far, I realize that my actions are driven less by the experiment and more by natural desire. I can also see how some of the kindness seems to bounce right back at me.

Too often we underestimate the power of a touch, a smile, a kind word, a listening ear, an honest compliment, or the smallest act of caring, all of which have the potential to turn a life around.

-Leo Buscaglia

Day 40

Nonnie called me at work and told me that she was getting the car washed. I noticed online that it cost $22. Keeping a family budget on track means trying to find a way to control the many small purchases/choices that a family is presented with. The problem is that when you try to prevent any single purchase you seem unreasonable. It is also a challenge because she was raised where her family regularly washed their cars on the weekends. I on the other hand am generally OK letting the rain handle that. I said that seems like an expensive car wash, but didn't overdo it. She asked where all the stuff I collected from the car was. I remembered that Sunday morning I took a trash bag and filled it up with all the shoes, toys and other items that were left in the car from our trip. In shock I realized that I threw it out with the trash. I just told her as sympathetically as I could that I think I threw it away. We went back and forth trying to determine if I really did that and what I remembered was in there. She was very disappointed.

I called her later and she told me that her journal from our time living in Spain was in there and that she just can't come to grips with the fact that it is gone. I offered to try to go to the landfill and find it but she said no. When I came home from work I told her how very, very sorry I was and gave her a long hug.

I told her that we had to leave for the boys' basketball practice in ten minutes. The boys weren't dressed for practice yet. Just then I realized that spaghetti noodles looked like they had just been placed in a pot of boiling water. I said we're going to have to eat when we get back. She said they can't go without eating and I said they could just have a snack to hold them over. She said again how much they needed to eat and I said, "I agree they should have eaten but the noodles should have been cooked before it was time to go." She was upset and explained all the things that have been going on. I calmly said, OK, let's eat and not worry about being on time. I tried to subtly hurry things along. Luckily we were only five minutes late.

When I came back from practice she told me that she found her journal from Spain. It was inside a binder that I had brought in earlier. She was so relieved and considered it a great blessing.

Love is a condition in which the happiness of another person is essential to your own.

-Robert Heinlein

Day 41

When I came home the kids gave me big hugs. Nonnie told one of them to go get my slippers. In a tone that suggested she wanted to let me relax, she said, "Here let me take your coat off," with a big smile on her face. I gave her a big hug and a kiss.

Later on that night when I was home from Cub Scouts and we were getting the kids to bed I was hobbling around exaggerating how tired I was. She said, "Ahh, come here" as she was sitting on the bed, gesturing for me to come give her a hug. After I hugged her for a few seconds, one of our kids came over and hugged us both.

You learn to speak by speaking, to study by studying, to run by running, to work by working; and just so you learn to love God and man by loving. Begin as a mere apprentice and the very power of love will lead you on to become a master of the art.

-St. Francis De Sales

Day 42

When I came home I said to Nonnie, "What can I do to make you happy" in a playful way to offer up my assistance to help with family duties. At around 10:30pm when I was really tired and still had a few other things to take care of before tomorrow Nonnie asked me to help put away the Christmas decorations that were piled up in the dining room. I told her not to say anything before I was finished and then told her that I was tired, it was past time when I should be going to bed and that even though I normally am willing to do family projects, I still had several things to do, and thought it could be done later in the week or on Saturday...but because I love her a lot and want her to be happy I would do it if she really wanted it done.

The fruit of Silence is Prayer

The fruit of Prayer is Faith

The fruit of Faith is Love

The fruit of Love is Service

The fruit of Service is Peace.

-Mother Teresa

Day 43

I answered the phone in a positive tone, "Hi Happiness!" Later on she asked me to help her with a diet program that I told her a few weeks ago that I did not think was a good idea. I said I would. It involved reading instructions and following a long process. I was tired and wanted to watch the NCAA national football championship, but helped her anyway. When we were done it was basically time for me to go to bed, but I said I wanted to catch at least a half hour of the game.

The truth is that our finest moments are most likely to occur when we are feeling deeply uncomfortable, unhappy, or unfulfilled. For it is only in such moments, propelled by our discomfort, that we are likely to step out of our ruts and start searching for different ways or truer answers.

-M. Scott Peck

Day 44

We received two free tickets to the Wizards NBA game and I took our oldest son who loves basketball. Nonnie asked me to bring the camera so I could take some pictures. When I finally arrived Warren said, "Dad, don't forget to take some pictures." I reached in my pocket for the camera and realized I left it in the car and knew Nonnie was going to be upset. I tried to make up for it by taking a couple pictures in Chinatown on the way home. When we came home Nonnie asked about the pictures and I told her I left the camera in the car and didn't get any at the game and that I was really sorry. She was disappointed but didn't say much about it.

We are all a little weird and life's a little weird, and when we find someone whose weirdness is compatible with ours, we join up with them and fall in mutual weirdness and call it love.
-Unknown

Day 45

I have been getting five or six hours of sleep since we returned from our trip and was starting to really feel run down. We agreed last night that we would each take two hour naps today. I got up with the baby a couple times early in the morning and I asked her if I could take the first nap. I had a great sleep until about 10:00am. I had a bowl of cereal and then we started into our "Saturday workday" jobs that Nonnie wanted the family to get done today. We cleaned bedrooms, bathrooms, the kitchen, vacuumed, and polished for about three hours. She was disappointed later in the day that we didn't get all the things done she wanted to that day. I asked what they were and tried to get them done. When we put the Christmas decorations away I gave her another big kiss under the mistletoe and asked if we should just keep it up all year, which we did.

I had just sat down to eat in front of the TV and mentioned that I forgot to grab a drink, not consciously trying to hint that she should do it. Nonnie quickly offered to go get one for me. She may have offered to do that without me doing the 100 Day Promise, but it likely makes it easier for her to think this way.

When she came home from the grocery store late at night I went downstairs to help her bring in the groceries and other bags. She had a good idea of a fun game we could play on our stay at home "date."

If every husband and every wife would constantly do whatever might be possible to ensure the comfort and happiness of his or her companion, there would be very little, if any, divorce. Argument would never be heard. Accusations would never be leveled. Angry explosions would not occur. Rather, love and concern would replace abuse and meanness.

-Gordon B. Hinckley

Day 46

I got up with the crying baby at around 7:00am and Nonnie came downstairs about 8:30am. I mostly fed and played with the kids until about 11:00am. When I was helping the kids get ready for church I walked in the bathroom and Morgan was smearing toothpaste on her face and I told her not to do that. She complained that she was just trying to get it off. Nonnie said I was being too hard on her. I said sorry, it just really looked like she was playing around. Then I helped her get the kids and all of her stuff out to the car. While she was gone I cleaned the kitchen and rearranged the storage room to make room for the Christmas boxes.

What is our response when we are offended, misunderstood, unfairly or unkindly treated, or sinned against, made an offender for a word, falsely accused, passed over, hurt by those we love, our offerings rejected? ... The nature of our response to such situations may well determine the nature and quality of our lives, here and eternally.

-Marion D. Hanks

Day 47

When Nonnie was upstairs putting the baby to bed she called down to me and asked me in a kind way how much longer I thought we should let the kids watch the show they were watching before bed. Since beginning this experiment, as I have become more considerate, so has she.

I was getting ready for bed and Nonnie came up and told me there was a TV show on that she really thought I would like and said I should come down and watch it.

Love is stronger than justice.

-Sting

Day 48

I left her a post-it note before I left for work on the computer wishing her good luck on her diet and that I knew she had the will to do it. I also sent her a link to a YouTube clip about Rocky training. She phoned me later and was really thankful for the support and motivation.

I left work just in time so I could pick up Warren as she had requested. I picked him up from Chess and got home just in time to get ready for basketball. She told me we needed to go get a toy for Morgan from the store because Nonnie's mom told us we could buy her something for her birthday. I told her we didn't have time and that we should do it tomorrow or some other day. She had promised Morgan that she could get it when I came home. I agreed to go quickly so they could still make it to practice. I drove fast, ran to the store, and raced back and got home just in time for them to leave for practice.

When she came home I asked her if she wanted me to help with the kids, etc. or whether one of us could watch a show we had talked about. She said I could go watch the show and she would handle the kids.

If a married couple with children has fifteen minutes of uninterrupted, non-logistical, non-problem-solving talk every day, I would put them in the top 5% of all married couples. It's an extraordinary achievement.

-Bill Doherty

Day 49

After scouts I was reminded that we had a meeting for the Cub Scout leaders. I had my son play with the other boys whose parents had to attend the meeting. At about 8:55pm Nonnie called my cell phone and said with a little irritation, "Where are you?" I explained that I forgot about the meeting, that I was sorry, and that I thought it would have been over by now and if it went much longer I would just leave.

When I came home I asked her how she was, rubbed her shoulders and asked her if there was anything I could do for her and kissed her several times on the cheek in a playful way. When I was getting ready for bed she came to get me to watch a short inspirational music video clip on the computer.

Trying to find lasting love without obeying God is like trying to quench thirst by drinking from an empty cup—you can go through the motions, but the thirst remains.

-John H. Groberg

Day 50

On my way home from work I called Nonnie to ask her how her day was. She didn't answer but when she called me back I answered saying, "Yeah, my happiness called me!" After finding out about her day and how everyone was doing I mentioned that I was starting to get a sore throat and needed to get some rest. She said she needed rest too. When I came home I asked her what I could do to help her. She asked me to make dinner and watch the baby. After everything had settled down she asked me if I wanted some herbal tea for my sore throat. I thanked her very much but said I really just needed to rest.

After I had just fallen asleep Nonnie came into my room and asked if I was asleep. I groggily responded, "A little." She then started talking about her thoughts about moving near her family or moving overseas. I listened a little and gave a few short responses but eventually said we could talk about it more tomorrow (as I was falling asleep). She then asked if we could say a prayer together and she said a beautiful prayer expressing gratitude for many things.

The weak can never forgive. Forgiveness is the attribute of the strong.

-Mohandas K. Gandhi

Day 51

I am really sick today. My ears and throat are sore and my whole body is weak and aches. I told Nonnie this on my way home from work and she expressed sympathy and said they would take care of me when I got home. When I arrived I laid down on the couch and Nonnie came and took my shoes and socks off and made me some herbal tea. I talked about how great she was looking and complemented her on her will power to follow through with her diet. I told her I didn't want to move from my spot on the couch so I could keep admiring her.

After dinner I sat down for a minute on the computer to pay some bills. As Nonnie came upstairs with the kids she asked if she could "check something real quick." I stayed out in the hall helping the kids get ready for the next ten minutes. I came in and asked who she wanted to read to the kids and the answer was inconclusive so I just went and read to them. After they were in bed I went back to the computer to pay the bills. Fifteen minutes later she came back and asked me if I could help her scan a picture and upload it somewhere. I was getting really tired of being interrupted and said OK, but after that I needed to be left alone. As she sat down to finish I was left standing again and went to do something else without complaining. Normally I would have made an issue of it, but in this case the Ghandi like approach led to a better result. Recently, while watching the movie *Ghandi* together I noticed there were several instances where the manor in which Ghandi's followers endured mistreatment softened the hearts of the public. In some instances they clearly had the means to put up a formidable resistance, but they were wise enough to realize where that would lead. She came back about fifteen minutes later saying she was sorry she took over the computer. I said it was no problem.

All things need watching, working at, caring for, and marriage is no exception. Marriage is not something to be indifferently treated or abused, or something that simply takes care of itself. Nothing neglected will remain as it was or is, or will fail to deteriorate. All things need attention, care and concern, and especially so in this most sensitive of all relationships of life.
-Richard L. Evans

Day 52

I was still feeling really sick with a sore throat and earache. I still went to work because it would not have been a good day for me to miss. As I was pulling out of the driveway I saw Nonnie standing in the doorway. I rolled down the window but could not hear her. I walked to the door and she told me that she had lost two pounds since she weighed herself. I told her that was amazing and that she is doing so awesome and gave her a big hug and kiss. She asked if the Dayquil medicine was helping me and asked if I wanted her to go grab some medicine for my sore throat.

When I called Nonnie on my way home from work I told her how bad I was feeling. She said when I came home I could just crawl into bed and rest.

I stopped off at the video rental store on my way home from work and called Nonnie to talk about what our options were. I mentioned three videos that looked good to me and wondered whether to mention one that I saw that did not interest me, but that I thought she would like. After she had picked one that I liked I said that there was one other movie, 500 Days of Summer. She said, "Oh I really wanted to see that." I joked that I knew I shouldn't have mentioned it and said I would get it.

Later on in the evening I was playing video games with the kids in the basement while the pizzas we made were cooking. Nonnie called down saying that two of them were finished. We kept playing thinking that one more was still cooking and that we didn't necessarily have to eat it immediately. After what seemed like a short time, Nonnie called downstairs and said the kids have to go to bed without eating because they didn't come upstairs. The kids were upset and I went upstairs and calmly tried to explain how I misunderstood the situation and was surprised we were at the no-eating point. She said they could eat.

We watched the movie and really enjoyed it. I think in some ways it reminded us of some of the feelings we have had about relationships over the years and reinforced how we feel we were meant to be together. I rubbed her feet during the movie.

Marriage must fight constantly against a monster which devours everything: routine.

-Honore de Balzac

Day 53

We got to sleep-in until one of the kids came in saying they had wet the bed. I slowly got up to handle it and Nonnie said she would get it. When she came back to bed we cuddled and I joked that it was a curse to be married to someone so pretty and that she had cast a spell on me.

We don't go on many dates. It seems we go out enough at night for other things, usually as a family, that I don't feel the urge to arrange other activities. I arranged for us to go to a play tonight, The Screwtape Letters, in Washington, DC. We have both heard the book on tape by C.S. Lewis and really liked it. This morning Nonnie told the kids in a genuine way how excited she was to go on a date with dad tonight.

Nonnie went upstairs about an hour and a half before the babysitter was supposed to come and after a few minutes I heard the shower come on. I was relieved that she was getting started early and was hopeful that we would make it to the play on time. About an hour and fifteen minutes later (fifteen minutes before the babysitter was supposed to come) she came down in a robe and wet hair. I was frustrated. I calmly said that I was really hoping we could leave not long after the babysitter came so we wouldn't have to rush all the way to the show. I also said there was no intermission and that walking in late to our front row seats would be difficult. She had been folding clothes and cleaning the rooms upstairs. She said she had to make her diet salad and had to eat right now. I said alright, but please do everything you can to help us leave as quickly as possible. I also asked what I could do to help her.

When we were getting dressed I asked Nonnie what she thought of a particular shirt for me to wear. Even though I thought it was a nice shirt she told me not to wear a casual work shirt and said I should wear a white shirt. In confusion I said, "A white shirt?" thinking that I usually only wear white shirts with a tie. Then she asked me to wear a suit. I knew this theatre was not all that formal and that a suit was unnecessary and I would probably be one of the only people wearing a suit. I suggested that and she said it would be fine and she wanted to dress up. I really didn't want to wear a suit. I stood there thinking for about twenty seconds, grabbed two of my suits and said, "Which one do you want me to wear."

We made it to the show on time and really enjoyed it. Waiting for the elevator at the parking garage we hugged and kissed and then when we were taking the elevator down had another romantic kiss. On the way home she really thanked me for the night and told me how much it meant to her.

When I eventually met Mr. Right I had no idea his first name was Always.

-Rita Rudner

Day 54

I heard the baby crying about 6:30am and got up to help her. I asked Nonnie what she thought she needed and Nonnie said the baby was probably ready to get up. Nonnie had gotten up a couple times in the night to help the baby. I took care of her and made pancakes for the rest of the kids when they woke up and let Nonnie sleep.

After the kids were in bed I was in the office on the computer checking email. Nonnie walked in for something and I asked her what she was doing. She said she was going to go fold laundry and then go to bed. I told her I would help her. When we were watching TV Nonnie said she wanted to watch an awards show. I had no interest in that but watched it with her for about an hour just to enjoy some time alone with her.

You have a clean slate every day you wake up. You have a chance every single morning to make that change and be the person you want to be. You just have to decide to do it. Decide today's the day. Say it; This is going to be my day.

-Brendon Burchard

Day 55

When we first woke up Nonnie asked me how my throat was. I said it was getting better but was still a little sore. She said it sounds like nothing a couple herbal teas couldn't fix. Her back was sore so I gave her a backrub. We had a great time at breakfast. I told the kids how lucky they were to have a mom that works so hard for them and how lucky I was to have married such a great lady.

Later I started telling Nonnie how much I liked and loved her. She said she loved me so much that she wasn't even angry at me for making her sick since she now had a sore throat. She even joked that she loves me more than the desserts she is dreaming of having while she is on her diet.

Love... What is love? Love is to love someone for who they are, who they were, and who they will be.

-Chris Moore

Day 56

I told Nonnie last night that I could take Sterling and Morgan with me on our Cub Scout field trip to the landfill/recycling center, but only if she had them ready by 6:00pm. I explained that it closed at 7:00pm and I had to pick up the other boys and drive 25 minutes to get there. I arrived home about three minutes to six and the kids were not ready with sweatshirts and shoes on and they were about halfway through dinner. Nonnie was in the middle of reading them a book as part of a reading program she does with them. After she finished reading the book I encouraged everyone to quickly finish eating and then to get dressed in a manner that wasn't too frantic.

I came home from playing basketball at about 11:00pm and cleaned the kitchen until about 11:30pm. Nonnie was very thankful. She also told me she had an appointment with the school counselor at 3:30pm and asked me to come home early. I mentioned that in the future it would help to have more advanced notice. She said she would but sometimes we are at the mercy of the school's schedule. I said I understood, but that sometimes I am not able to come on short notice, but I would try to make it.

He who wants a rose must respect the thorn.

-Persian proverb

Day 57

I came home at 3:00pm so she could go to the meeting and she was really happy when I arrived and thanked me again. I went to H&R Block tonight to work on my taxes. A little while after I was done Nonnie pulled up to the curb and was on the phone. In the past she would walk in and sign the papers while I stayed with the kids in the car until she came back out. When she arrived she was on the phone and didn't get out of the car. After a few minutes I motioned for her to come in and she held her finger up for me to wait. After a few more minutes the tax lady asked, "Is that her?" I said, "Yes." A few minutes later I was standing at the door waiting and the tax lady asked if she was coming in and I said, "Yes…but you can't make a rose bloom, it blooms when it wants to" and smiled. Nonnie finally came in and stayed on the phone in the lobby for another three or four minutes. When we left I decided to not make an issue out of it.

After we came home and were finishing putting the kids in bed I asked if there was anything I could do for her. She was happy to hear that. I checked email late tonight and saw Nonnie had posted a message on my Facebook wall about how happy she was to have received flowers.

Love does not consist of gazing at each other, but in looking together in the same direction.

-Antoine de Saint-Exupery

Day 58

We were watching TV and Nonnie said she needed a drink of water and asked me if I wanted one. I said that I would go get it for her. She said it was alright and that she would get it.

Nonnie updated her Facebook status today saying, "My husband bought me flowers the other day and let me tell you it has made my entire day, just looking at them makes me and the home feel elegant and beautiful! Go and buy your girl flowers (or yourself). One teeny tiny tip, there is a time and place for roses but you can never go wrong with Tulips!!" The woman likes flowers.

Love is to let those we love be perfectly themselves, and not to twist them to fit our own image... otherwise we love only the reflection of ourselves we find in them.

-Unknown

Day 59

When Nonnie and I talked on the way home we agreed that I would go to the video store on the way home from work and get some things for her at the grocery store. I told her to keep her cell phone handy if she wanted to have a say in the video. She said she would. I called her several times but she didn't answer. I felt like I should get whatever I wanted so I picked out one that I liked. I decided to try to make her happy even though she didn't answer and also got one for her that I thought she would like. When I came home she asked what I picked out. I told her and added that she didn't answer so I didn't know what she wanted. Then I brought a smile to her face when I told her I got one for her anyway and she said I was great.

I knelt down to say a prayer before I got into bed. I asked Nonnie if we could pray together. I prayed about things I thought she was concerned about and expressed gratitude for the good things in our life.

Kindness can become its own motive. We are made kind by being kind.

-Eric Hoffer

Day 60

The baby started crying around 6:05am and I asked Nonnie what she thought the baby needed. She said just the pacifier and she should go back to sleep. I got up and gave her the pacifier and then went back to sleep. Around 6:10am the baby started crying again and I asked Nonnie what she thought the baby needed this time. She said she could tell the baby was really awake this time. I said I would handle it and took the baby into the basement so I could change and feed her and keep her quiet until Nonnie woke up. I woke her up around 7:45am to get the kids dressed so I could take them to Sterling's basketball game. I took all the kids to Sterling's basketball game at 8:00am while Nonnie went to a church event.

When we came home Nonnie called and asked me to do something around the house. I said, "Sure, no problem." She said thank you in a tone that showed appreciation for not making an issue of it. I told her a couple times how impressed I was with the determination she has in following through with her diet. Despite a couple frustrating moments I hugged and kissed her a few different times during the day. We snuggled together when we watched a movie and I rubbed her back.

After enlightenment, the laundry.

-Zen proverb

Day 61

When I woke up this morning I wasn't feeling well. Nonnie and I woke up about the same time and she asked if I could make pancakes. I said I was getting a sore throat and a cold sore and felt like I should rest. I said I would make the pancakes but asked if I could take an hour nap afterwards and then she could take a nap after me. She said sure.

I asked her later what she thought the best time today was for me to work on my Cub Scout planning. She said that was such a nice way to ask. I came upstairs later and she was in bed. She said she didn't feel well and was frustrated with how much needed to get done in the house. I rubbed her back for a while and then folded the laundry.

I bought a rose last night and hid it outside. When she was in the shower I put it in a tall glass and put it in the cup holder in her car with a note saying I loved her. She really liked that.

I take nothing for granted. I now have only good days or great days.

-Lance Armstrong

Day 62

Tonight I stayed home with Bethanie while Nonnie took the two boys to their basketball practice along with Morgan. While she was gone I did the dishes, opened some mail, organized the office, took laundry downstairs and fed the baby. I was feeling really tired when she came home and knew I still had to finish the pinewood derby car with Warren, pay a few bills, prepare an activity for Cub Scouts tomorrow, respond to a couple emails, respond to a teaching position vacancy and get to bed as soon as possible. When Nonnie came home around 8:30 she said she wanted to do an activity with the family since we try to do it once a week. I said I was happy to do it however she wanted, but that I wanted her to be aware of what I had ahead of me tonight. She said something about me trying to get out of it which frustrated me a little. I said that I was willing to do it; I just wanted her to listen so she could factor my situation into how long we spent with the family. I was in a bad mood for a few minutes because of her reaction but tried not to let it show too much because I wanted to end it there. Not too long after I was over it.

Love is an act of endless forgiveness, a tender look which becomes a habit.

-Peter Ustinov

Day 63

When I came home from work Nonnie asked me how work was while she dealt with one of the kids and was cleaning up. I said it would take me about thirty seconds and asked if she had that much time to listen, partially joking about how she gets distracted when she is working or dealing with the kids. She said she did. I started to tell her something about the name of my new department and she interrupted saying she already knew that. I didn't think she would have been able to name it if I had asked her what it was so I asked her something else about the name. She told me to come over and give her a hug. She skillfully employed what I like to describe as an "asymmetric response," where you engage with someone in a way they weren't expecting. Even though I was setting up for a little argument, I didn't have a defense to her request.

Nonnie told me tonight that she broke her diet and ate the rest of one of the kid's burritos. It was day 19 of a 21 day diet. I had been complimenting her regularly on how much determination it took to do what she is doing and that when she is done it will have been a real accomplishment. Now that she fumbled I didn't know what to say that would show love. I just said it was too bad and that it was OK and agreed when she said at least she had lost a certain number of pounds. I tried to help her realize it was a small setback and that she really has been great. I told her it is like tripping in a marathon, it may have set you back a little but you definitely cannot just give up and sit by the side of the road. It seemed to help a little.

She decided later to go to the store. I mustered the will to clean the kitchen especially because I thought in the final stages of her diet she would not want to have to be around food. I was almost in bed when she came home and I went downstairs to ask if she needed a hand bringing things in from the car.

It's the action, not the fruit of the action, that's important. You have to do the right thing. It may not be in your power, may not be in your time, that there will be any fruit. But that doesn't mean you stop doing the right thing. You may never know what results come from your action. But if you do nothing, there will be no result.

-Mohandas Gandhi

Day 64

We were going to go ice skating when I came home from work. When I came home Nonnie said it was too late for us all to go and she asked if I would just take the kids while she stayed with Bethanie. When I came home she really thanked me for giving her time to work on the presentation she is giving on Saturday and gave me a big hug and kiss. After the kids went to bed she went out to run some errands. She asked me if I would put away the food, but asked if that was too much to ask in a very nice way. I said it was no problem at all.

Commitment unlocks the doors of imagination, allows vision, and gives us the right stuff to turn our dream into reality.

James Womack

Day 65

When I came home it was around 9:00pm and all the kids were still awake, except the baby. Nonnie was on the phone and I just handled the bedtime routine. After that I asked if there was anything she needed me to do. Nonnie also showed me the new baby car seat and wristwatch that she purchased. I wasn't excited, as she was, about the great deal she got on the watch and didn't think we really needed a new car seat, but chose not to make an issue of it.

If we do not hang together, we shall surely hang separately.

-Thomas Paine

Day 66

I stayed home from work today so she could fly out of town to speak at a parenting seminar. In the morning before she came downstairs I replaced all the lights in the kitchen that she had mentioned earlier this week. I also told her I would vacuum the stairs that she wanted done because Bethanie crawls on them so often.

Nonnie said she wanted Sterling to stay home from school today. He seemed fine to me and we debated it a little. A few minutes later she came to me in a very calm and respectful way and explained more about what she was worried about. I said that I was only partially persuaded but that because of the great way she handled the situation I didn't even care anymore. At that moment I was really just so happy to see her choose to handle a tense situation with such amazing patience, respect and self-control.

On the way to the Baltimore airport I recalled a time when I drove up that way when we were first married when I worked an extra job at night to make a little extra money. She mentioned the other extra jobs I had done to help us make it through those early years. She hugged my arm and put her head on my shoulder and told me what an awesome husband I was and how much she loved me.

If you're trying to achieve, there will be road blocks. I've had them; everybody has had them. But obstacles don't have to stop you. If you run into a wall, don't turn around and give up. Figure out how to climb it, go through it, or work around it.

-Michael Jordan

Day 67

I knew it would mean a lot to Nonnie if I made some progress around the house. I spent a couple hours going through mounds of papers in the office and straightening things out. I had the kids clean their rooms and the basement while I folded laundry and cleaned out my closet. I also shoveled the five inches of snow we had from the driveway, walkway and sidewalk and took the kids to their basketball game and two birthday parties. We talked later on the phone and I asked all about her trip and her speech and was very happy for her that it went well.

Character consists of what you do on the third and fourth tries.

-James Michener

Day 68

Before we left to pick Nonnie and the baby up at the airport I made a final effort to straighten things up. I had the kids make their beds and put toys and shoes away. She was coming in at 4:00pm so I estimated that it would take her about 20 minutes to exit the plane and get her luggage. Traffic was a little slower than I expected and I arrived at 4:33pm. I had tried to call her a few times but she didn't answer. When I picked her up she was frustrated that I was late and was in a bad mood. I said that I was really, really sorry she had to wait for so long and explained what my plan was and what happened. It took some effort, but after a few minutes I had her smiling and was kissing her hand. She also explained later how terrible the flight had been and how fussy Bethanie was in the airport making it even harder to wait.

When we came home she was really happy with how much work I had done around the house. I carried her suitcase upstairs and she laid on the bed for a rest. I rubbed her feet for a few minutes while we talked about the past two days. I then told her I would take care of feeding the kids and that she could just take some time and rest.

For where your treasure is, there will your heart be also.

-Jesus, Matthew 6:21

Day 69

I called Nonnie from work and asked how her day was. She said I made it go very well because I did so much work over the weekend and was very appreciative. The kids were home from school today and she said she could really enjoy having them home.

It was my week to take the boys to basketball practice and I told Nonnie that I was only going to be home just in time to take them and that we would need to leave around 5:30pm. I tried to call her a few times on the way home from work to remind her to make sure they were ready but she didn't answer. When I came home at 5:40pm the boys were playing with a friend in a fort they made in the living room. They weren't dressed and had not had dinner. We disagreed a little about what to do next, but finally got them to practice. When I came home I stood at the top of the stairs and was still a little bothered about what had happened before basketball practice. I paused for a moment and thought about how easy and justified it would be to let my frustration show and continue the negative cycle. Instead, I walked up to her and gave her a big hug and a kiss and had a great night.

Nothing in the world can take the place of Persistence. Talent will not; nothing is more common than unsuccessful men with talent. Genius will not; unrewarded genius is almost a proverb. Education will not; the world is full of educated derelicts. Persistence and Determination alone are omnipotent. The slogan 'Press On' has solved and will always solve the problems of the human race.

-Calvin Coolidge

Day 70

It was snowing hard on the way home from the pinewood derby. I arrived home first and shoveled the driveway and opened the garage door for her since the garage door opener wasn't working.

After we came home from the pinewood derby we put the kids to bed and Nonnie went into the office to get on the computer. I sat on the futon to talk to her. While I was talking she turned around and surprised me by asking if I wanted a footrub. Nonnie does a lot of nice things for people, including me. However, this caught me off guard. I smiled as I considered the inner changes that must have occurred for her to offer to rub my feet at that time.

Often the difference between a successful marriage and a mediocre one consists of leaving about three or four things a day unsaid.

-Harlan Miller

Day 71

It snowed about five inches last night. When I woke up for work I saw on the internet that school was closed. I looked outside and saw that the street had not been plowed. I decided to leave a few hours late to give them time to clear the roads. I laid back down for a few minutes and the baby woke up. I took the baby downstairs and fed her. I then started making hash browns and eggs. Nonnie came downstairs before I could take them up to her in bed. After a few minutes she told me I should go upstairs, relax, and take a bath.

Nonnie was putting pictures on Facebook and I happened to see that one was of me. I asked if I could look at the picture first. When I tried to open the picture I ended up canceling the four pictures she was already set to upload. When I tried to pull the pictures back up the computer started going slow. She was frustrated but she came back to me ten minutes later and in a very kind way apologized for overreacting.

We who lived in concentration camps can remember the men who walked through the huts comforting others, giving away their last piece of bread. They may have been few in number, but they offer sufficient proof that everything can be taken from a man but one thing: the last of the human freedoms – to choose one's attitude in any given set of circumstances, to choose one's own way.

-Viktor Frankl

Day 72

When Nonnie and I talked on the way home from work I told her that the tax refund came in and how happy I was. I mentioned that I paid some bills that needed to be paid with the money. She said something about not liking that we ended up using that money to pay bills. I resisted the urge to explain how some of the things she has spent money on were part of the reason we were in this situation and just basically agreed with her.

Nonnie asked me if I could buy a snow shovel on my way home for someone who was stuck at home with sick kids. We are expecting a snowstorm tomorrow. She also asked me to pick up some blinds for the dining room. I told her I would be happy to if she really wanted, but I recommended that we wait because the dimensions have to be measured very carefully and that I was worried that her passing them to me over the phone would likely result in an inaccurate cut. She thought we could get the measurements right and I agreed to do it.

When I came home we hugged and kissed for a couple minutes. I joked again about the love curse that I was under. She showed me the gifts she bought the kids for Valentine's Day. Even though I thought it was a waste to buy the kids Valentine's Day gifts (I have never heard of parents doing that) I only made a comment that it was strange to do that but I didn't overdo it.

I never saw love as luck, as that gift from the gods which put everything else in place, and allowed you to succeed. No, I saw love as reward. One could find it only after one's virtue, or one's courage, or self-sacrifice, or generosity, or loss, has succeeded in stirring the power of creation.

-Norman Mailer

Day 73

Today we were excused early from work because the forecast was calling for 20 to 28 inches of snow and the storm had already started. People were rushing to get home. Nonnie asked me to stop off at the craft store to pick up a lollipop making kit. Not bread, milk, or things that people run to the store for, but, a lollipop making kit! I joked about how ridiculous it was for me to go there when everyone else was "scrambling" for shelter but I did it without any serious complaint. The people at the store must have wondered what I was up to. I also came home with a bouquet of tulips which she was very excited to see.

When it was time to start dinner I said, "So what should I make for dinner?" She said that was such a nice way to ask.

Start by doing what's necessary, then what's possible; and suddenly you are doing the impossible.

-Saint Francis of Assisi

Day 74

Today we had about 26 inches of snow. I spent a few hours outside clearing the driving and walkway while the kids played around me for some of the time. Nonnie knocked on the window with Morgan at her side and I wrote in the snow, "I Heart U" and she smiled.

When I was in the basement with the kids I told them to clean up a little in the basement and to start with putting the books on the shelf. As I was following up with them Nonnie said I was too hard on them and we disagreed about how it should be done. A few minutes later I went upstairs to feed the baby and heard the country song, "I Get Carried Away" by George Strait. I turned it up really loud and called down to everyone in the basement, "Hey guys, this song tells how I feel about Mom."

After I was in my pajamas I remembered that I had to go in the back yard and check the vent from the dryer. I just put my wet boots on without lacing them and went out. The snow was up to my thighs and was filling up my boots. When I came back I said that I had made a huge mistake by not lacing up my boots and made a little scene as I removed my boots and brushed the snow off. Nonnie kindly asked what she could do to help me.

When Nonnie was helping Morgan say the family prayer before bed she told Morgan to pray that Dad wouldn't hurt too much after all the work he did today.

We are, each of us, angels with only one wing, and we can only fly embracing each other.

-Luciano DeCrescenzo

Day 75

I got up with the baby and made waffles for everyone. Nonnie had been up with the baby a few times during the night. Some neighbors came by today with some brownies for us. After they left Nonnie said, "Kindness comes back." I agreed and thought that was a succinct way of saying something that has been said before and also captures a big part of my experiment.

Today was a day of fun and hard work. I shoveled more of the driveway as the snowplows buried us in. Nonnie really worked hard around the house and about three or four times throughout the day we hugged and kissed when we were standing around each other. I joked later about how I was the baby whisperer the way the baby responds to me. I jokingly asked her if she thought I was the wife whisperer. She said, "Sometimes." Later on in the evening she asked me if I wanted a back massage which I really appreciated after dealing with the snow.

Every person in this life has something to teach me—and as soon as I accept that, I open myself to truly listening.

Catherine Doucette

Day 76

Nonnie asked me to do Yoga with her and the kids. I told her no because my back really hurt from shoveling all the snow. She said it would help relax my back and I said I didn't think so. She asked me to at least come down in the room with them. When I came downstairs I said I would do it with them. We had a fun day in the snow and doing things around the house. These snow days have been fun, but also add an unexpected challenge to my 100 Day Promise by forcing us to confront our different priorities for extended hours of free time.

Work joyfully and peacefully, knowing that right thoughts and right efforts will inevitably bring about right results.

-James Lane Allen

Day 77

The federal government was closed again today due to another snowstorm coming today. I slept in until around 8:00am which was really nice. After breakfast I took Morgan to buy groceries and get more videos from Blockbuster. I picked movies that I knew Nonnie would like more than ones that I would prefer.

I made a frozen skillet lunch for Nonnie and I, while the kids were eating. About twenty minutes later Nonnie called downstairs asking if I had lunch yet in a way that sounded like she was showing concern. I told her that I made lunch for us and she was thankful.

Nonnie asked me to work on the shadow boxes in the dining room. Since we moved in the house a few years ago we have had a long list of projects we have wanted to get done. Naturally, she was more concerned about finishing them quickly, but I have told her I would just take one at a time. We had been working on the dining room, including putting up crown molding. She wanted shadow boxes up and even bought the wood to help me along, but I have been sidetracked by what I consider to be a busy life. I explained that the garage had snow and water all over the floor and that it would be difficult to cut the pieces. After she explained how important it was to her due to an upcoming event I said I would do it.

We were sitting in the basement with the kids and Nonnie said, "Oh I have to call and set up violin lessons for Sterling." We had not discussed whether or not we would do this although I have heard her say it would be nice for the kids to take certain musical instrument lessons. She stopped and looked over and said, "I mean I need to call and get the information about the lessons so we can discuss it." I complimented her on remembering that and she smiled.

I rubbed her feet while we watched the movie and had a fun discussion after. Before we went to bed I put the new blinds up in the dining room.

Love and you will be loved, and you will be able to do all that you could not do unloved.

-Marques de Santillana

Day 78

We all had another snow day home from school and work. I fed the baby while Nonnie took a shower and got ready for the day. She told me she was getting a cold and I told her she should take it easy and rest and that I would take care of things. I told her later how I enjoyed being around her.

In the middle of the long day inside the boys and I started up the Wii. About five minutes later Nonnie told us to turn it off because she wanted them to work and do some other activities. I told her we had just set it up and that only one of us had played so far and asked if it could wait a little. She said they had watched TV enough for today and needed to do something else. I could have resisted but decided to go with the flow of what she wanted.

We were watching *The Time Traveler's Wife*. It came to the part where the wife was upset that he was gone for two weeks. I said, "Don't take the bait man, just do something romantic." Nonnie chuckled and said, "You're giving romance advice?" I said, "Ouch, I'm going to write that down." She said she was just kidding and that I actually was romantic.

I argue very well. Ask any of my remaining friends. I can win an argument on any topic, against any opponent. People know this, and steer clear of me at parties. Often, as a sign of their great respect, they don't even invite me.

-Dave Barry

Day 79

Nonnie and I decided to get a babysitter and go see a movie. I opened the car door for her which I don't normally do when the kids are there and we held hands walking into the movie. I joked about weird things that were happening around us and she jokingly complained that I let a huge family get in line in front of us. She kept leaning into me affectionately while we waited in line.

On the way home we decided that we should take the kids somewhere fun that afternoon. Later we decided that I would stay home with the baby so I could get a few things done. After Nonnie returned from taking the babysitter home she came to me and said she was really tired and asked if I would take them. I said yes and went bowling with the kids. On the way home I stopped off at the store to get a few things for Valentine's Day. I normally only get flowers and maybe something else small. This time I got her a candle I knew she wanted, two CDs I thought she would like, and a Kitchenaid mixer she had asked for last week which I previously said no to. Although it would seem to violate the rule against buying appliances for Valentines or Mother's Day, I thought she would really like it because she has talked about how she wants to get into baking a lot more. A lady at the store laughed when she heard me say to my three kids, "Which color do you think mom would like more, the red or the white one?" They all said the red one and one of them said, "The red one, for Valentine's Day."

    Before I went to bed I asked Nonnie if there was anything I could do for her. She asked me to bring up a load of clean laundry from the basement to our bedroom upstairs. As I was brushing my teeth I saw her carrying another load of laundry up the stairs. I walked halfway down the stairs and took the laundry the rest of the way.

This is the art of courage: to see things as they are and still believe that the victory lies not with those who avoid the bad, but those who taste, in living awareness, every drop of the good.

-Victoria Lincoln

Day 80

Today was my first day back to work in a week. As I was tying my shoes and Nonnie was getting ready she asked me if she could run to the grocery store before I left for work. I told her I was just about to leave. She said she needed some things for a Valentine's Day party she was going to throw for the kids today who were still home from school. She had invited some of our kids' friends. I told her it wasn't good to try to handle things like this right as I was leaving for work. I then asked her what exactly she needed and said I would just go to the store for her. She was extremely thankful.

When I came home from work I asked her all about her day and the party. I told her how great she was to make things so fun for our kids. I told the kids in front of her how lucky they were to have such an amazing mom. We had a fun time getting the kids ready for bed. When we sat down to watch TV I felt peaceful and glad to be sitting next to her.

Your task is not to seek for love, but merely to seek and find all the barriers within yourself that you have built against it.

-Jalāl ad-Dīn Muhammad Rūmī

Day 81

While she was out this morning I wrapped the Valentine's Day gifts and hid them around the house for her to find throughout the day.

When she came home she had a number of things she had purchased at Lowes. The most problematic was a fan that she had purchased that she wanted installed in the living room where there currently was not an overhead light fixture. She said she had already talked to our neighbor who said he could help. I didn't like that she asked our neighbor to help me this afternoon without talking to me first. I also didn't like her assuming I would just drop whatever else I had wanted for the day and spend it working on that. I told her I was annoyed, but that I would get over it if she could give me some sense that she understood why I didn't like it. I said what if I came home with a crochet kit and told her I wanted her to knit me a sweater that afternoon and that I had asked a lady to come help her. She said when I put it like that she could see my point. I grumbled for a few minutes and tried hard to shake my annoyance. I had to knock about six holes in the ceiling to drill holes in the joists and drop the wires into the light switch. Since I was inexperienced at this it took me seven hours to complete the project and I finished after 10:00pm. We were both so happy when we hit the light switch and it worked.

While I was working on the fan she found the first gift, the Valentines music CD. It was in the refrigerator. She said, "Wow, you really have the love bug." She was so excited because she said she has been thinking a lot about trying to find some good Valentine's music. Later Morgan asked Nonnie to read a book to her in a tent she had set up in the basement. She found the second present when she went in to read it. She said it was so romantic to find it that way. It was a cupcake candle I heard her say that she liked. She came up and said how awesome it was and said I was showing her up this Valentine's Day. The kids didn't really keep the secret and told Nonnie she should look in her room. She came downstairs with a big present I put in her closet. She was so excited and couldn't believe it. She had one of the boys videotape her opening it and when she saw what it was she squealed with excitement and ran over and gave me a big hug and kiss. She found the other CD in the microwave a couple of hours later. She was so excited and kept commenting on how great the idea was and how much she loved it.

After the kids were in bed and I finished the fan we ate some fruit and chocolate with the fondoo set and took turns answering fun questions that were in a jar. We have done this a few other years in the past. All in all, it was a very nice evening.

There is no such thing as a 'self-made' man. We are made up of thousands of others. Everyone who has ever done a kind deed for us, or spoken one word of encouragement to us, has entered into the make-up of our character and of our thoughts, as well as our success.
-George Burton Adams

Day 82

This morning I slept in while she made a fun Valentine's Day breakfast for the family. While we were eating I told the kids in a fun way how that fan represented how much I loved their mom. I explained how I wasn't excited that she bought it, wasn't excited about her asking for our neighbor's help, and wasn't excited about installing it. I said, "Because I love your mom so much I worked on it anyway for seven hours until it was finished." Nonnie smiled.

Today the 100 Day challenge wasn't so challenging. The kids were in bed and I was watching the Olympics. She came down with a baked potato she had made and asked me if I wanted one. We sat very closely and enjoyed being with each other.

We come to love not by finding a perfect person, but by learning to see an imperfect person perfectly.

-Sam Keen, from To Love and Be Loved

Day 83

This morning we both woke up to the sound of the baby talking. Nonnie sat up on the side of the bed and stayed for a moment. I asked how she was doing and she said, "Tired." I said I would feed the baby and she said, "No, I've got it." I then said that whatever she needed help with just let me know. She came back into bed for a few minutes to cuddle.

Nonnie wanted to post a wedding photo on her Facebook profile for Valentine's Day as others had been doing. She wrote describing when we met, were engaged and married. She finished saying, "…and still on our honeymoon;)….Happy Valentine's Day All!"

I stayed home with the baby while Nonnie took the other three kids to Monticello for President's Day. I really am amazed at how driven she is to give our kids the richest life possible. When Nonnie came home after 6:00pm she told me her plans to make a special President's Day dinner of clam chowder in a bread bowl. She said she needed some things from the store. I made a mild attempt to convince her that we should just do something simple but then offered to go to the store for her. I then helped her efforts to have a candle lit dinner where she read to them about different presidents and had food associated with a few presidents. I was tired and didn't initially share the same passion but realized afterwards what a great experience it was.

The most basic and powerful way to connect to another person is to listen. Just listen. Perhaps the most important thing we ever give each other is our attention...A loving silence often has far more power to heal and to connect than the most well intentioned words.

-Rachel Naomi Remen

Day 84

Today I called Nonnie from work to find out how her day was going. She told me she was really tired and wanted to sleep. I told her that I would stay home from basketball tonight so she could relax. She told me later tonight how much it meant to her.

After the work of the evening was over I went downstairs to watch TV. Nonnie came down a little later and laid her head on my shoulder and we had a nice night talking about the kids and goals we were thinking about.

Our greatest glory is not in never failing, but in rising up every time we fail.

-Ralph Waldo Emerson

Day 85

When Nonnie and I talked on the phone at work she told me that she was thinking more about how I worked so hard to put the fan in. She said especially when she thought about my analogy to me coming home and asking her to knit me a sweater. She said, "You are a champion, champion, of all champions. You should be walking tall, proud, and pleased with yourself for what you were able to accomplish."

When I came home I was very excited to see all my kids and gave them big hugs and kisses as they ran to the door. I gave Nonnie a lot of hugs and kisses as she was making dinner. I told her how happy I was and thanked her for working so hard for our family.

I helped the kids clean the basement, get ready for bed, read to them and got Nonnie a drink. I asked her what I could do for her tonight and she asked me to fold laundry. I said I would and said I would also take care of the kitchen.

I decided to take a break in the basement before I cleaned the kitchen and watch the Olympics. Nonnie called down about 45 minutes later and said with a little annoyance, "You didn't put the food away…the cheese was left out." I said I was sorry and didn't realize the cheese was still out. I went upstairs and she had Bethanie in her arms who was crying with an ear infection. We worked on helping the baby for the next hour and I held her for a long time after that to help her fall asleep.

Only in love are unity and duality not in conflict.

-Rabindranath Tagore

Day 86

I woke up at 5:40am so I could leave for work in enough time for me to be home for Nonnie to go work out at the gym. When I arrived I found out she wasn't going anymore because she wasn't feeling well. I joked a little about how that is information that would have been nice to know before I rushed out of the office. She said she still needed me because of how she was feeling.

When I came home from work we were making dinner in the kitchen and working on Valentines for the kid's classes. Morgan asked with a smile on her face, "Mom, why did you leave the mistletoe up?" Nonnie said, "so I could have another reason to kiss dad," then we kissed.

The baby had just woken up so I said I would stay in the basement play area with her while the other kids worked on their Valentines. A few minutes later, Nonnie asked me with some exasperation to come upstairs and help her deal with the kids who were being a handful. Warren then said, "Fire in the hole!" causing Nonnie to laugh.

Constant kindness can accomplish much. As the sun makes ice melt, kindness causes misunderstanding, mistrust, and hostility to evaporate.

-Albert Schweitzer

Day 87

As I was driving home from work I realized how excited I was to come home and be with my family. I called Nonnie and told her and she thought that was really romantic. I had been thinking during the day about what I could do this weekend that would mean the most to Nonnie and I recalled how she has talked about how the garage is a mess. When I told her on the phone she was happy to hear it.

As we were walking upstairs Nonnie handed me the baby. I played around like I didn't know why she was handing me the baby then took her. As I was getting the baby dressed for bed I asked Nonnie what I could do for her tonight that would mean the most to her. She said that was really nice and asked rhetorically about my sudden desire for kindness. I asked her when she noticed a change. She said, "Since about five seconds ago." I thought it was funny since technically it had been 87 days. After the kids were sleeping I asked Nonnie all about her day and showed concern for the trials and complimented her on the successes.

Let us not hurt the ones we love the most by selfish criticism! In our families, small arguments and petty criticisms, if allowed to go unchecked, can poison relationships and escalate into estrangements, even abuse and divorce. .... We cannot afford to let such dangerous passions ruminate--not even one day."

-David E. Sorensen

Day 88

We woke up a little late this morning to get Sterling to his basketball team pictures at 7:30am. I knew we had to leave in ten minutes and I asked Nonnie to get him dressed and I would get ready to take him. I restrained a little frustration as it was time to leave and she was carefully ironing his uniform and then asked me to go get hair gel to put in his hair.

We went to the International House of Pancakes after his basketball game for breakfast which is one of Nonnie's favorite things.

After refereeing a basketball game and then going to Warren's basketball game I worked with the boys around the house. We cleaned the garage, bedrooms, bathrooms and vacuumed the stairs. After I finished vacuuming the upstairs Nonnie noticed it was on the wrong setting and asked if I would do it again. I said sure, even though I normally would have argued that it was good enough.

While we were eating dinner I asked the kids what they thought was nice about each member of the family. When they were talking about me Nonnie said, "Dad helps me out A Lot", with emphasis.

After the kids were in bed Nonnie asked me to help her download and print things out for church tomorrow. She was feeling really sick, had a sore throat, and was annoyed that the computer wasn't working right. Nonnie realized she needed new ink cartridges and asked me if I had it in me to go to the store to buy some new ones before it closed. I said, "Sure." While at the store I decided to get Nonnie a card. I found a really funny one with some monks with scared expressions on a roller coaster. I wrote, "Nonnie, I thought this card was just crazy enough that it just might work. I just wanted to get you something to make you laugh and let you know that I think you're amazing in every way. Love, Brian." I decided to leave it somewhere where she would find it.

When I came home Nonnie thanked me for getting the cartridges. When I was putting the cartridges in she put her arm around me and said she was really sorry for being impatient with something I was trying to help her with earlier. I hugged her back and I said it was no problem. When she came downstairs an hour or so later she sat down next to me and held my hand.

Self-esteem creates natural highs. Knowing that you're lovable helps you to love more. Knowing that you're important helps you to make a difference to others. Knowing that you are capable empowers you to create more. Knowing that you're valuable and that you have a special place in the universe is a serene spiritual joy in itself.

-Louise Hart

Day 89

Nonnie was feeling even worse this morning so I kept all the kids downstairs so she could sleep. She wasn't sure she could handle her project at church and I helped her work through some options and even offered to do it for her. I basically took care of the kids all day and tried to get her what she needed. I hid the card I wrote last night in a book that was sitting on her nightstand. Nonnie mentioned that this has been a great week because she can't stop thinking about the fan I installed in the living room.

Lead your life so you wouldn't be ashamed to sell the family parrot to the town gossip.

-Will Rodgers

Day 90

Nonnie was just as sick today and she asked me to stay home from work to take care of the kids. I brought her some herbal tea in bed. When I was taking care of the baby downstairs I decided to leave the TV off because I knew Nonnie would appreciate it.

When I was running a couple errands she called me with a great proposal for a better way to handle our finances which really surprised me.

Around bedtime I gave the kids the option of getting ready for bed or watching the Olympics with me. Sterling chose to watch the Olympics. Nonnie said they had been watching TV all day and didn't think they should be watching more. I resisted the urge to explain all the other things they had done and just said, "OK, we'll keep it short."

I don't really like going to the grocery store late at night, especially when I could have gone earlier in the day. She asked me to go and I very reluctantly said, "Yes" and cringed as the list grew and grew. After it reached a certain point I said I didn't want to be that guy that has five people with one item behind me in the only line that is open while I buy a weeks worth of groceries. She cut if off there. When I came home Nonnie gave me a heartfelt thank you.

We must develop and maintain the capacity to forgive. He who is devoid of the power to forgive is devoid of the power to love. There is some good in the worst of us and some evil in the best of us.

-Martin Luther King, Jr.

Day 91

Nonnie asked me to stay home again today and I could see she was in real pain. The whole day my heart went out to her as I could see each swallow was torture. She would periodically shiver as well. Unfortunately we couldn't get a doctor's appointment until tomorrow. I worked really hard throughout the day taking care of everyone.

We had some visitors from church stop by offering assistance and I explained about Nonnie's doctor's appointment and they offered to take Morgan to preschool and have her over after preschool was over. They also offered to bring us dinner tomorrow and anything else we needed. At Cub Scouts tonight a number of other people offered to help us out.

When everyone else was going to bed I talked to Nonnie about tomorrow. She asked if I could stay until after her morning appointment. I told her I truly sympathized with her, but wanted to explain my situation at work and then we could make the best decision. After I realized the predicament she was in I told her I would stay.

A man is a little thing while he works by and for himself; but when he gives voice to the rules of love and justice, he is godlike.

-Ralph Waldo Emerson

Day 92

I have been sleeping on the couch the past few days so I wouldn't get sick as well. At 4:45am I went up to take care of the crying baby. As I was closing the door, Nonnie came walking down the hall and told me she hasn't been able to sleep. I told her I was sorry to hear that and made sure she could sleep in as late as possible before her doctor's appointment. When she came into the kitchen she was very grateful.

When Nonnie came home from the doctor's appointment she was still in a lot of pain, wincing with every swallow. She said there wasn't any medication for the type of infection she had. I knelt beside her and held her hand as she lay on the bed. I told her how sorry I was that she was hurting and asked if I could do anything for her. I offered to stay home the rest of the day but she said that it was fine for me to go.

When I came home Nonnie had set out the food that friends from church had brought for dinner. I thought it was nice of Nonnie to ask me if she could make me a plate in light of how bad she was feeling.

I decided to empty the dishwasher and straighten up as much as I could so that her day will be as easy as possible tomorrow while I'm at work. When she came downstairs she was hurting a lot and gave me a very humble and grateful hug.

Kind words can be short and easy to speak, but their echoes are truly endless.

-Mother Teresa

Day 93

I called Nonnie in the middle of the day to see how she was and she was really hurting. She called me around 2:00pm and I could hardly understand her and she sounded emotional and in a lot of pain. I told her I would come home right away, but she said I could wait a couple of hours. Nonnie asked me to buy an onion on the way home because her family uses them to help earaches. I wanted to joke about the onion and ask if she wanted me to bring frog legs, tree moss, or anything else for the brew, but I decided not to. At the store I bought her a small pot with tulips, her latest favorite flower.

When I came home I just hugged her and told her how sorry I was that she was so sick and asked what I could do. She said there was nothing I could do, so I just took care of things as best I could. Later on in the evening she went with a friend to the urgent care center because the regular doctor said to wait and see if she got better by Monday before she ran additional tests and didn't offer her any remedies. When Nonnie came in the house she had a smile on her face and I was so happy for her that she finally had some relief. They gave her a shot to reduce the swelling in her throat area.

Love is more than just a feeling: it's a process requiring continual attention. Loving well takes laughter, loyalty, and wanting more to be able to say, "I understand" than to hear, "You're right."

-Molleen Matsumura

Day 94

I accidentally took Nonnie's phone with me to work so we communicated over email. I asked her if she wanted me to bring anything home. She replied, "Flowers, take two? No, forget about that..it's more romantic when it comes out of the blue :)…Your Adoring Wife." She asked me last night if she could use the tulips I brought to give to someone as a gift.

When I came home I found Nonnie on the computer and I rubbed her shoulders while we talked. Nonnie had the chairs set out of the kitchen as though she was preparing to clean the kitchen. A little later I offered to sweep and mop the floor.

Serving others need not come from spectacular events. Often it is the simple daily act that gives comfort, uplifts, encourages, sustains, and brings a smile to others.

-Michael J. Teh

Day 95

I got up with the baby at 6:00am, fed the kids, and got Warren ready for his basketball game so Nonnie could rest from her illness. I took Warren to his game, worked with the family cleaning and then went to work on the moldings.

When I was working on the moldings in the dining room Nonnie came to me and said she wanted to run some ideas she had for the day by me and see if they worked with what I wanted to do. I usually introduce my proposals that way and was surprised to see her do the same thing.

I cleaned the kitchen, then took Morgan to her birthday party and got a present on the way. I brought the two boys with me and we had some fun before we picked her up again. When we came home we watched the second half of a basketball game, then I fed Bethanie and got her ready for bed.

When I arrived at the store I noticed an item on the shopping list Nonnie made, "Apples (Good Ones)." I had mentioned a few years ago that I try hard to pick the best ones they have and don't need to be reminded or have her suggest I pick bad fruit. One time I even half jokingly told her if she ever wrote that on a shopping list again that item might be "forgotten." I thought about not buying the apples, but realized that was foolish and decided to not even bring it up again. I also bought her the granola without the raisins because she doesn't like them and some tulips. When I came home and went downstairs she handed me the TV remote and put her head on my shoulder.

Hope is definitely not the same thing as optimism. It is not the conviction that something will turn out well, but the certainty that something makes sense, regardless of how it turns out.

-Vaclav Havel

Day 96

I got up with the baby around 6:00am so Nonnie could get some extra rest. She has still been feeling sick, even though her sore throat is feeling better. When she came downstairs she brought me my slippers. Although I rarely wear slippers I thought it was a kind gesture.

Nonnie commented several times throughout the day how great the dining room looked. It was mostly finished but needed a second coat on the moldings. She agreed to wait on talking about the next project until we finished this one and then went on about me being an awesome husband.

Reflect upon your present blessings, of which every man has plenty; not on your past misfortunes of which all men have some.

-Charles Dickens

Day 97

I got up with the baby at 5:30am when she started crying, changed her diaper and got her back to sleep. I told Nonnie I could stay for a while in case she wakes up again, but if I did it would make it hard for me to leave work early enough to pick up Warren from chess practice. She said thanks, but that I could go.

When I was planning a trip for work I made an extra effort to arrange it in a way that she could come. I called her from work to tell her it worked out and she was really happy. She also commented how great the house projects looked and how I was such a hard worker.

When I came home I said, "Just because you're sick doesn't mean we can't hug and kiss," and I pressed my cheek to hers. I had asked her if she would be up for going on a date Friday night, but some friends offered to repair the ceiling holes from when I wired the fan. I asked her if we could do it on Thursday instead and she asked what the surprise was. I said there was no surprise; I just thought it would be nice to go out. I took the kids to basketball practice and bought a chess set for Warren at the store on the way home.

When we were eating ice cream with the family, Warren said something funny and Nonnie kept looking at the fan in the living room and held her smile for a long time. I told her she looked happy and she said she was. I asked if it was the fan and dining room. She said, "It's everything." I cleaned the kitchen before I went to bed to make things as easy as possible for Nonnie, especially since she is still feeling bad.

You can have everything in life you want, if you will just help other people get what they want.

-Zig Ziglar

Day 98

When I answered the phone this morning at work Nonnie, responded, "You are so great," and went on to explain how wonderful it was to come down and see a clean kitchen and said she told Morgan, "I am so lucky I married your dad." Nonnie then went on to say something that really amazed me. She said, "Last night I had the distinct thought that I am too dependent on you, I thought, 'I'm liking this guy too much. I need him and want to be around him.'" She went on to say, "This doesn't give me the upper hand. I am going to have to change things real quick," joking about the vulnerability she felt about that. I was happy and grateful to hear her say that realizing that everything I have tried to do the past 98 days has led to something great.

When I came home from work Nonnie was completely worn out and I wasn't able to help her because I had to get ready for Cub Scouts. In addition to Warren, I took Sterling and Morgan with me to give her a break.

You bring out the best in yourself by looking for the best in others.

-Gene Bedley

Day 99

I was pulling out of the driveway around 5:50am on my way to work and realized I forgot something and went back inside. As I was leaving the house Nonnie came down the stairs saying she heard me leave and was wondering why I came back. She gave me a great goodbye hug.

I was in training all day today. I called her during a break to see how she was and to let her know I would be away from my desk. She thanked me and said she was having a hard time. I made sure to leave as soon as I was able to help her out.

I had prayed for something to happen to give this 100 Days a nice ending. When I arrived home about an hour earlier than normal Nonnie cried out, "Yeah, Dad is home!" Morgan and our babysitter, Chloe, were working on a poster for school that really surprised me and made me smile. It said, "100 Days Give Me Warm Fuzzies." I was puzzled for a moment wondering if somehow they found out about what I was doing. I had a huge smile on my face as I asked what it was for. Morgan's preschool was having them create something to celebrate their 100th day of pre-school and Nonnie came up with that slogan. I thought it was quite a coincidence in light of my 100 Days of trying to completely show love and concern.

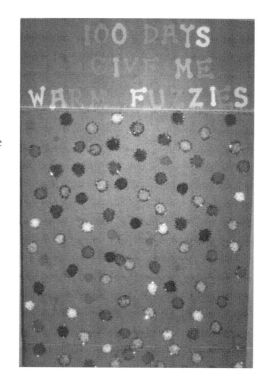

Nonnie called me when I was in the grocery store line asking me to pick up a few more things. I said, "Oh, actually I am already in the checkout line." She said, "Oh, would you mind getting them anyway?" I said with some exaggerated kindness, "Sure, no problem, in light of what I am prepared to do for you, it's not even worth mentioning." She said, "Ahhh, thanks."

He felt now that he was not simply close to her, but that he did not know where he ended and she began.

-Leo Tolstoy

Day 100

  This morning when I woke up Nonnie thanked me for the note I left her last night—I had gone to bed before her and left a note on her pillow thanking and complimenting her. I left a little later today because I had to take the car to get repaired. I took the trash out and as I was walking towards my car I saw Nonnie standing in the front doorway smiling. She saluted me and I smiled and accepted her salute by flipping my head to the side.

  I called her from work to discuss the final plans for our dinner tonight. I told her I had something I wanted to talk to her about at dinner. I didn't tell her what it was, but did give her a clue. I said, "100 Days Give Me Warm Fuzzies."

Conclusion

As I look back on the past 100 Days, I see things I could have done better. What I did is by no means a model for other families, as each relationship is different. People from different cultures and backgrounds may find some of the things I did unusual. I simply tried to do what I thought would make her happiest, as I understood it, in our unique circumstances.

This is the seemingly illogical message: you can find your happiness by seeking your spouse's happiness first. You don't have to surrender all your personal goals and desires. There still needs to be frequent discussions about personal and family goals; and compromises need to be reached. Sometimes saying nothing may give you a short-term gain, but not contribute towards long-term happiness. Perhaps that is one of the greatest challenges, having the wisdom to know what things are worth discussing. You need to be able to express your feelings, however, you don't have to vocally judge everything that happens. If you put your spouse's happiness equal to or above your own, you will initiate a chain reaction that will shape both of you in ways that could happen in no other way. Great things can begin to happen when even one spouse begins to think this way. Imagine what would happen if both spouses really put the other's concerns above their own, or at least give them loving consideration when balanced against the overall needs and goals of the family.

There are some people who would take your love and kindness for granted. This isn't the sole answer to every problem that can arise in a relationship. However, I think it will be very difficult to get to the place you want to go without having this frame of mind. In addition, I believe most people will be changed when they receive selfless love, sustained over a period of time.

What happened to Nonnie?

It is impossible to fully observe on the outside what really happens when someone loves you. Nonnie was noticeably happy as a result of these 100 days. She showed more consideration when she asked me to do things and as we were making plans. The kindnesses seemed to create a buffer in front of the occasional inconsiderate things I said. Nonnie seemed to have more "wind in her sails" to move forward with her many goals and take on the world. She noticed and appreciated the change and even wondered a couple times if I was "dying or something" which always made me laugh.

What happened to me?

I can say that my love for her increased. For some reason I wanted to be around her more and it was liberating to think selflessly. I was happier as I concentrated on her happiness. At first it took effort, but toward the end it started to become second nature. I believe an important purpose of life is to develop attributes of humility, self-control, patience, and kindness. I definitely exercised and strengthened those abilities.

Was it worth the work?

Yes. When I think of the vision I have of our family in the future I realize how amazing the reward of a loving family will be over the years. When I think of those who are unable to pull it off I marvel at how tremendously sad it is. I believe strong families are essential to avoiding the many problems that our society faces. How much more successful, prosperous and happy the world would be if more people could think a little more this way. Some people believe that God has a plan for their life that includes their spouse. Even if you don't, you likely made a covenant with Him to love the one you married. It is a sacred trust.

What does it take?

Above all else it takes a strong person who can get over a negative encounter without dwelling on it and move on. Relationships will spiral down or up. You have to be able to break the downward spiral by doing something kind or outrageously considerate even if your sense of justice drives you the other direction. Once you understand the consequences/rewards of deciding whether to love, it is easier to find the will. Prayer is also an important means to find the attributes that you lack. You may have to find a new level of maturity and self-control.

Ways to Love:

Everyone has their own way in which they want to be loved. Some authors have called this the "love language." For a family with four young kids an important part of a wife's love language will likely be helping with the housework and the kids. Nonnie loves flowers and thoughtful notes or indications that I was thinking of her. Most people yearn to be heard and complimented. Spouses like to be supported in their goals and priorities. A positive attitude is important. Critiques should be rare and with the utmost respect. Sometimes you have to say sorry even if you think you were only 5% at fault. Sometimes it is better to just say you are sorry and give her a hug without giving an explanation about what you were thinking. It is also important to forget about equity, such as who had a harder day or whose turn it is. The real beauty comes when both sides approach the relationship with this perspective. It only takes a little more energy to increase the water temperature from 211 to 212 degrees. Yet when that happens a reaction takes place causing the water to boil and release its power. I believe most marriages remain just below the point where they take off and that with just a little more determination to love they can find the true rewards that a marriage can bring.

Epilogue

by

Nonnie King

Every so often after school I would walk over to my dad's office across the street to wait for him to finish up and take me home. Oftentimes he would put me to work stacking boot boxes of the family owned western wear business or helping in the accounting and merchandizing offices filing mounds of paper work. One day when I arrived he had me sit down in the company's boardroom and list all the qualities I wanted in a future husband. I didn't find it odd in the least since my dad was ever the planner/dreamer and if it got me out of work I was all too happy to oblige. There in that boardroom, being all of 14 years old, I came up with a list that would shape and determine my future. After every date, starting from age sixteen on, I would come home, write my date's name down and go through 'The List' to compare what qualities he had and what he was missing. Needless to say, I approached marriage, rather, the person I was marrying, with the kind of thought, time, and preparation that most people put into a choosing a college, career, car, and home purchase combined.

When I met Brian it was easy to see that he not only fit 'The List' perfectly, he was the list. Soon after we were married, kids entered the picture.

Without realizing it my focus soon shifted from being wife to being mom. My thought, or rather justification, was he is already finished (I had the list to prove it) and now we needed to concentrate our efforts on helping these babies turn out just as great. When the pangs of guilt would surface as to whether or not I was treating Brian and our marriage with the same time and energy I was giving my children, I would quickly come to my defense that there would be time enough for us after all these babies were properly raised and we could sit back and enjoy each other as we watched the fruits of our labor. Of course, then I would turn all my time and focus back to him. For now, however, my focus should be on our children.

Why then if my focus was primarily on my children would I be sitting at the intersection of Linton Hall and Sudley Manor, 10 years into our marriage, feeling overwhelmed with more love and peace than I had ever felt in my life? The answer was simple. Even though I didn't know it at the time, it was Day 97 of Brian's love experiment and it was working. Nothing had changed; our finances were the same, our house was the same, our children were the same, but everything was somehow different. When Brian told me at dinner a few nights later what he had done, or rather been doing, I was surprised to say the least. At no time during these 100 days did I suspect anything like this. True, at times I wondered if he was dying and even told my sister, "Either he is dying or I'm dying, but something is definitely up."

When Brian told me this experience had been so great and life altering that he wanted to share it with the world, I was just as excited. After what I experienced I couldn't help but want others to benefit in the same way. Then I read the daily entries. I believe I said something to the effect of, "I would rather be hit by a train" than let the world see what a horrible wife I am. You see, I knew these were not stellar years in the marriage department but I had no idea how bad I was until it was staring me in the face for 100 days. I saw myself as Day 41 when I put the slippers on his feet, but one day out of 100 does not a habit make. I was grateful to see it so I could start to make the necessary corrections and learn from it but I was quite sure I could do that without the glaring *help* of friends, family, or the entire world. Then after sharing what Brian had done with some of my friends I got a different reaction than what I expected. I expected a "How nice," or even a "Wow!" What I got instead were several women wanting to not only read the draft, but do this same experiment for their husbands. I saw such hope and excitement in them to improve their marriages that I soon overcame my insecurities and realized this experiment was bigger than me. If it changed even one other marriage for the better, well by all means, I'd gladly be hit by a train (metaphorically speaking of course).

What this experiment did for me was show me that I have someone by my side willing to do something so extraordinary in such ordinary circumstances. One of my favorite quotes he uses is "Marriage must fight constantly against a monster which devours everything: Routine." It is every girl's fairytale to have the brave knight burst through the burning doors of the castle, slay the three-headed monster, rescue her from the tower and ride off into the sunset. What Brian did for me, for our marriage, is equivalent to just that. He stopped that monster, Routine, and turned it on it's head. He changed the course of our marriage by demonstrating the power of kind and selfless acts, even though he didn't have to…After all, it wasn't even on The List.